AF556152

Hospitality Automation and Computerisation

HOSPITALITY AUTOMATION AND COMPUTERISATION

Gopal Verma

CENTRUM PRESS
NEW DELHI-110002 (INDIA)

CENTRUM PRESS
H.O.: 4360/4, Ansari Road, Daryaganj,
New Delhi-110002 (India)
Tel: 23278000, 23261597, 23255577, 23286875
B.O.: No. 1015, Ist Main Road, BSK IIIrd Stage,
IIIrd Phase, IIIrd Block, Bengaluru-560085 (INDIA)
Tel: 080-41723429
Email: centrumpress@gmail.com
Visit us at: www.centrumpress.com

Hospitality Automation and Computerisation

First Edition, 2013

ISBN 978-93-81460-03-0

PRINTED IN INDIA

Printed at Balaji Offset, Delhi.

Contents

Preface

The hotel salesperson of today has a great many technological innovations to work with that are intended to make the sales job easier and more effective, as well as produce more bottom line results for the hotel. Technology provides several communication tools the salesperson might be using to improve interaction with the customer and with the hotel. Customer communication tools would include: e-mail, e-mail attachment capabilities, voice mail and cell phones. Additionally, the salesperson would use e-mail internally between departments within the hotel, as well as with sources of sales leads from regional sales offices, convention and visitors bureaus, etc. In order to make the job more efficient, the salesperson relies on technology for administrative activities such as word processing and developing spreadsheets of sales results.

It is also important that today's salesperson be able to access information from a variety of locations beyond the traditional office environment including working at home or when travelling. The technology tools available for administrative tasks in these contexts include laptop computers and PDAs or handheld computers. Of course, to be able to do all of the administrative functions, as well as customer research using technology, access to the Internet needs to be as quick as possible raising the issue of high speed Internet access capabilities. In order for the salesperson to be more effective in selling there are technology tools designed to assist with presentations, to do research on customers, and to make it easier for the customer to access information on the hotel.

Presentations to customers today typically include PowerPoint presentations to the customer. The customer can also access more information on the hotel through the World Wide Web, which can also be a source of generating lead activity to the hotel through requests for proposals (RFPs).

The Internet is used in the sales department for customer research and finding contact information for organizations the salesperson wishes to solicit for future business. Additionally, meeting planners are now expressing a desire to be able to use technology to plan meetings using diagramming software of meeting rooms such as Meeting Matrix, Optimum Settings and Room Viewer. Hotels need to recognize this and react accordingly to stay up with the technology usage of the customer. All of the above tools form the basis for the hotel sales technology tools analysis in this study.

As mentioned, the focus is on the salesperson's perception of how important each tool is in daily selling activity and whether it is performing as would be expected. Thus, we examined the gap between the importance of computerization and technology tools available to the sales force and their satisfaction level with those tools in performing their sales responsibilities. The importance of understanding the various relational variables at the individual, organizational, and contextual construct levels to hotel automation as conditions to the extent of automation adoption in hotels was discussed. The purpose was to empirically test the relationship between selected independent variables under the three constructs to the dependent variable, extent of automation in the front office of hotels. Technological advancements in recent decades have precipitated significant change in the world's labour force, at every level. Growth and decline of different sectors, and change in the occupational structure of the workforce have been the subjects of extensive research. Much literature discusses the impact of technological development and globalization on the organizational structures of the labour force. However, there remains a need for a "shop floor" perspective of changes in work processes over time.

The aim of the book is to put researchers engaged in different areas of research on a common platform so as to be benefited by the current state of knowledge in the field of this subject.

Author

1

Introduction

Tourism is travel for recreational, leisure or business purposes. The World Tourism Organization defines tourists as people who "travel to and stay in places outside their usual environment for more than twenty-four (24) hours and not more than one consecutive year for leisure, business and other purposes not related to the exercise of an activity remunerated from within the place visited". Tourism has become a popular global leisure activity. In 2008, there were over 922 million international tourist arrivals, with a growth of 1.9% as compared to 2007. International tourism receipts grew to US$944 billion (euro 642 billion) in 2008, corresponding to an increase in real terms of 1.8%.

As a result of the Late-2000s recession, international travel demand suffered a strong slowdown beginning in June 2008, with growth in international tourism arrivals worldwide falling to 2% during the boreal summer months, and this negative trend intensified as international tourist arrivals fell by 8% during the first four months of 2009. Thereafter this declining trend was exacerbated in some regions due to the outbreak of the influenza AH1N1 virus.

Tourism is vital for many countries, such as Egypt, Greece and Thailand, and many island nations, such as The Bahamas, Fiji, Maldives and the Seychelles, due to the large intake of money for businesses with their goods and services and the opportunity for employment in the service industries associated with tourism. These service industries include transportation services, such as airlines, cruise ships and taxis, hospitality services, such as accommodations, including hotels and resorts, and entertainment venues, such as amusement parks, casinos, shopping malls, various music venues and the theatre.

Definition

Theobald (1994) suggested that etymologically, the word "tour" is derived from the Latin 'tornare' and the Greek 'tornos,' meaning 'a lathe or circle; the movement around a central point or axis.' This meaning changed in modern English to represent 'one's turn.' The suffix -ism is defined as 'an action or process; typical behavior or quality' whereas the suffix -ist denotes one that performs a given action. When the word tour and the suffixes -ism and -ist are combined, they suggest the action of movement around a circle. One can argue that a circle represents a starting point, which ultimately returns back to its beginning. Therefore, like a circle, a tour represents a journey that is a round trip, i.e., the act of leaving and then returning to the original starting point, and therefore, one who takes such a journey can be called a tourist.

Hunziker and Krapf, in 1941, defined tourism as people who travel "the sum of the phenomena and relationships arising from the travel and stay of non-residents, insofar as they do not lead to permanent residence and are not connected with any earning activity." In 1976, the Tourism Society of England's definition was: "Tourism is the temporary, short-term movement of people to destination outside the places where they normally live and work and their activities during the stay at each destination. It includes movements for all purposes." In 1981, the International Association of Scientific Experts in Tourism defined tourism in terms of particular activities selected by choice and undertaken outside the home.

The United Nations classified three forms of tourism in 1994, in its "Recommendations on Tourism Statistics: Domestic tourism", which involves residents of the given country travelling only within this country; Inbound tourism, involving non-residents travelling in the given country; and Outbound tourism, involving residents travelling in another country. The UN also derived different categories of tourism by combining the three basic forms of tourism: Internal tourism, which comprises domestic tourism and inbound tourism; National tourism, which comprises domestic tourism and outbound tourism; and International tourism, which consists of inbound tourism and outbound tourism. *Intrabound tourism* is a term coined by the Korea Tourism Organization and widely accepted in Korea. Intrabound tourism differs from domestic tourism in that the former encompasses policymaking and implementation of national tourism policies. Recently, the tourism industry has shifted from the promotion of inbound tourism to the promotion of intrabound tourism, because many countries are experiencing tough competition for inbound tourists.

Terminology

Vacation, in English-speaking North America, describes recreational travel, such as a short pleasure trip, or a journey abroad. Most of the rest of the English-speaking whose of recent British or European descent, rarely say *going on holiday*. People in Commonwealth countries also use the phrase, *going on leave.*

Canadians often use *vacation* and *holiday* interchangeably referring to a trip away from home or time off work. In Australia, the term can refer to a vacation or a public holiday.

International Tourism Receipts

In 2008, there were over 922 million international tourist arrivals, with a growth of 1.9% as compared to 2007. International tourism receipts grew to US$944 billion (euro 642 billion) in 2008, corresponding to an increase in real terms of 1.8% on 2007. When the export value of international passenger transport receipts is accounted for, total receipts in 2008 reached a record of US$1. trillion, or over US$3 billion a day.

History

Wealthy people have always travelled to distant parts of the world, to see great buildings, works of art, learn new languages, experience new cultures and to taste different cuisines. Long ago, at the time of the Roman Republic, places such as Baiae were popular coastal resorts for the rich. The word *tourism* was used by 1811 and *tourist* by 1840. In 1936, the League of Nations defined *foreign tourist* as "someone travelling abroad for at least twenty-four hours". Its successor, the United Nations, amended this definition in 1945, by including a maximum stay of six months.

Leisure Travel

Leisure travel was associated with the Industrial Revolution in the United Kingdom – the first European country to promote leisure time to the increasing industrial population. Initially, this applied to the owners of the machinery of production, the economic oligarchy, the factory owners and the traders. These comprised the new middle class. Cox & Kings was the first official travel company to be formed in 1758. The British origin of this new industry is reflected in many place names.

In Nice, France, one of the first and best-established holiday resorts on the French Riviera, the long esplanade along the seafront is known to this day as the *Promenade des Anglais*; in many other historic resorts in continental Europe, old, well-established palace hotels have names like the *Hotel Bristol*, the *Hotel Carlton* or the *Hotel Majestic* – reflecting the dominance of English customers.

Many leisure-oriented tourists travel to the tropics, both in the summer and winter. Places often visited are: Cuba, the Dominican Republic, Thailand, North Queensland in Australia and Florida in the United States.

Winter Tourism

Winter Sport

A winter sport is a sport commonly played during winter. As a formal term, it refers to a sport played on snow or ice; informally, it can refer to sports played in winter that are also played year-round, such as basketball. The main winter sports are ice hockey and figure skating, sledding events, such as luge, skeleton, and bobsleigh, skiing (Alpine and Nordic) and snowboarding. Other common winter sports include skiboarding, monoskiing, skwal, and snowmobiling.

List of Winter Sports

Note: an asterisk indicates that a particular sport is included in the Winter Olympic Games, as of the 2010 Vancouver Olympics.

Ice skating

- Figure skating
- Short-track speed skating
- Speed skating
- Synchronized skating

Skiing

- Alpine skiing
- Biathlon
- Cross country skiing
- Freestyle skiing
- Mogul skiing
- Newschool skiing
- Nordic combined
- Ski archery
- Skiboarding
- Skibob
- Skijoring
- Ski jumping
- Snowshoe
- Speed skiing
- Telemark skiing.

Sledding

Sports that use sleds going down ice tracks or pulled by something:

- Airboard
- Bobsled

- Dogsled racing
- Ice Blocking
- Luge
- Skeleton
- Work racing.

Snowboarding

- Alpine snowboarding
- Boardercross
- Freestyle snowboarding
- Slalom

Snowmobiling

- free style
- snow-cross
- recreation
- cross country
- hill climbing.

Recreational Sports

Some 'sports' are competed (or simply enjoyed) on a more casual basis, often by children:

- Building snowmen
- Ice boating or sailing
- Ice fishing
- Ice swimming
- Shinny
- Snowball fight
- Tobogganing.

Team Sports

- Bandy
- Broomball

- Curling
- Ice hockey
- Ice stock sport
- Ringette
- Sledge hockey - (Winter Paralympic Sport)
- Snowball fight - (Last one standing)
- Snowman building - highest one.

Notable Winter Sport Resort Regions

- Alps
- Andes
- Appalachian Mountains
- Balkan Mountains
- Carpathian Mountains
- Karkonosze Mountains/Sudeten mountains
- Lapland
- Rocky Mountains
- Snowy Mountains
- Swiss Alps
- Whistler.

Notable Winter Sporting Events

- Winter Olympic Games
- Asian Winter Games
- Winter Paralympic Games
- Winter Universiade
- Winter Dew Tour.

Major ski resorts are located in the various European countries (e.g. Austria, Bulgaria, Czech Republic, France, Germany, Iceland, Italy, Norway, Poland, Sweden, Slovakia, Spain, Switzerland), Canada, the United States, Australia, New Zealand, Japan, South Korea, Chile and Argentina.

Mass Tourism

Mass tourism could only have developed with the improvements in technology, allowing the transport of large numbers of people in a short space of time to places of leisure interest, so that greater numbers of people could begin to enjoy the benefits of leisure time.

In the United States, the first seaside resorts in the European style were at Atlantic City, New Jersey and Long Island, New York.

In Continental Europe, early resorts included: Ostend, popularized by the people of Brussels; Boulogne-sur-Mer (Pas-de-Calais) and Deauville (Calvados) for the Parisians; and Heiligendamm, founded in 1797, as the first seaside resort on the Baltic Sea.

Adjectival Tourism

Adjectival tourism refers to the numerous niche or specialty travel forms of tourism that have emerged over the years, each with its own adjective. Many of these have come into common use by the tourism industry and academics. Others are emerging concepts that may or may not gain popular usage. Examples of the more common niche tourism markets include:

Introduction to Fish Tourism

Fish tourism is part of the wider context of marine ecotourism and involves special tourism services associated to fishing and aquaculture and related customs and traditions.

Fish tourism is part of the wider context of marine ecotourism and may involve the embarkation of persons (who are not members of the crew) on fishing vessels for recreational-tourism purposes, as well as the accommodation, catering and general provision of special tourism services associated to fishing and aquaculture and related customs and traditions.

The development of fish tourism may be perceived as an employment diversification opportunity aiming to help regenerate coastal communities, and fishermen in particular, that are experiencing economic hardship as a result of the decline of their income from traditional fishing activities. Moreover, fish tourism may propagate eco-awareness and the principles of sustainable development on both the parties involved, operators and customers, fishermen and tourists.

The need for such diversification in coastal regions -and the fishing communities in particular- has been long recognized by many national and international authorities, recommending that the inshore fisheries sector should be encouraged to pursue opportunities for diversification in addition to safeguarding traditional fishing activities.

Such diversification, which is considered a priority by the EU, has been successfully implemented in many costal regions of the EU. In all cases, apart from the economic, societal and demographic reasons that set the base for the development of fish tourism in a region, a supportive and comprehensive legal framework is required.

Fish tourism may be able to help regenerate fishing communities, and address low incomes, low levels of investment, high unemployment, out-migration, and so on.

Moreover, fish tourism is thought to offer a special opportunity to achieve environmentally sound, sustainable development – development that will help to meet the needs of the present generation without damaging the resource base for future generations.

It can also make a contribution to the objective of 'balanced spatial development' set out in the European Spatial Development Perspective (ESDP), by addressing regional disparities through sustainable use of the region's indigenous potential.

Case Studies

A Short Description of Fish Tourism in Italy and Ireland

What is the Case of Italy?

Italy is closely related to the sea as there are 7,600 km of coastline and many inland waters (lakes and rivers). There are more than 16,000 fishing vessels, the majority of which are costal and small scale fishing vessels, largely affected by diminishing fish stocks. The increasing rate of unemployment has led to the development of alternative forms of occupation (professional diversification) and fishtourism activities in particular.

Apart from sport fishing of large pelagic species like swordfish and tuna, pescaturismo has developed over the past few years, combining demonstration of fishing activities as well as participation. The Italians made one step further developing ittiturismo which is a form of agrotourism practiced in coastal areas with emphasis given on fishery related traditions and customs. This kind of tourism provides a chance to the local fishermen to improve their income and to the tourists to discover the local fishing culture and explore the coastal areas.

Fish tourism has developed not only close to the sea, but also in inland areas, in communities where inland water fishing is practiced, such as in lagoons, lakes and rivers. There are big national federations like FIPS (Federazione Italiana Pesca Sportivo) and KONI (Italian Olympic Commission) which organize occasionally sport fishing games across Italy. Carp, roach, trout, pike, eels are some of the species abundant to the lakes of Garda, Como, Iseo, Lago Maggiore, Trasimeno, Bracciano and Bolsena and of course salmon and trout to the rivers. Due to the tendency of the recreational fishermen to participate in such fishing activities, it is very likely that Pescaturismo will expand also to the inland waters.

What is the Case in Ireland?

The picturesque landscape of Ireland and the long fishing tradition of the country has aided the development of recreational fishing both in marine and inland waters.

The Bord Failte (Irish Tourism Organization) in cooperation with the Central Fisheries Board and the National Organization for the Fishery inform recreational fishermen on aspects concerning the legal framework covering the recreational fishing. There are many organizations chartering small vessels to recreational fishermen for inshore fishing, deep-sea fishing and wreck fishing.

These types of fishing excursions are provided additionally to sightseeing ones. Recreational fishing is also allowed from the shore (shore angling) and to inland waters using fly-fishing or coarse angling. The high rate of environmental and nature conservation awareness of the Irish people has led to the development of many organisations whose mission is to educate fishermen and such issues.

In Ireland, there is a union of 21 specialized recreational fishing centres called "The Great Fishing Houses of Ireland", offering integrated thematic vacations, including subsistence and athletic activities like game fishing. Tourists pay a certain fee to fish or charter a fishing vessel and the rate depends on the season (high or low). The services are highly rated and provided by professionals of tourism management. Moreover, tourists are being informed on aspects concerning the local culture and tradition about fishing, also receiving maps and informative material.

Agritourism

Agritourism, as it is defined most broadly, involves any agriculturally-based operation or activity that brings visitors to a farm or ranch. Agritourism has different definitions in different parts of the world, and sometimes refers specifically to farm stays, as in Italy. Elsewhere, agritourism includes a wide variety of activities, including buying produce direct from a farm stand, navigating a corn maze, picking fruit, feeding animals, or staying at a B&B on a farm.

Agritourism is a form of niche tourism that is considered a growth industry in many parts of the world, including Australia, Canada, the United States, and the Philippines. Agritourism overlaps with geotourism, ecotourism, and culinary tourism. Other terms associated with agritourism are "agritainment", "value added products," "farm direct marketing", and "sustainable agriculture".

Agritourism in the United States

Agritourism is widespread in America. Agritourists can choose from a wide range of activities that include picking fruits and vegetables, riding horses, tasting honey, learning about wine and cheesemaking, or shopping in farm gift shops and farm stands for local and regional produce or hand-crafted gifts.

According the USDA, Cooperative State, Education and Extension Service, "Tourism is becoming increasingly important to the U.S. economy. A conservative estimate from the Federal Reserve Board in Kansas, based on 2000 data, shows that basic travel and tourism industries accounted for 3.6 percent of all U.S. employment. Even more telling, data from the Travel Industry Association of America indicate that 1 out of every 18 people in the U.S. has a job directly resulting from travel expenditures."

Through the Small Farm Centre at the University of California, "Agricultural tourism or agritourism, is one alternative for improving the incomes and potential economic viability of small farms and rural communities. Some forms of agritourism enterprises are well developed in California, including fairs and festivals. Other possibilities still offer potential for development." The UC Small Farm Centre has developed a California Agritourism Database that "provides visitors and potential entrepreneurs with information about existing agritourism locations throughout the state."

In Western North Carolina, the organization HandMade in America is using agritourism to develop their local economy and craft trades, and to educate visitors about agriculture practices. On the web site, *Hand Made in America,* they look at agritourism as a niche market [that] not only assists communities with solutions to help diversify their economic base, but it also helps our regional urban centres and increasingly suburban populations to understand the important role that farming and rural life plays in our history, by highlighting the need for it in our contemporary society.

Agri-tourism projects reinforce the need to support local growers and sources and allow the visitor to experience what it is to be part of the land.

The publication *Promoting Tourism in Rural America* explains the need for planning and marketing your rural community and weighing the pros and cons of tourism. According to the publication, local citizen participation is helpful and should be included in starting any kind of a tourism program. Citizen participation in planning tourism can contribute to buliding a successful program that enhances the community.

Additional websites that promote and publicize agritourism in the United States include Rural Bounty, founded by agritourism consultant Jane Eckert, Sleep in the Hay, a nationwide directory of farm stays, and Farm Stay USA, a blog that profiles farm stays and tracks agritourism news.

Reasons for Popularity

People have become more interested in how their food is produced. They want to meet farmers and processers and talk with them about what goes into food production. For many people who visit farms, especially children, the visit marks the first time they see the source of their food, be it a dairy cow, an ear of corn growing in the field, or an apple they can pick right off the tree.

Agritourism was featured in the satirical NBC television comedy series *The Office* in the episode entitled "Money" from season 4. The character Dwight Schrute lives on a beet farm, and in this episode reveals that he has opened a B&B in his farmhouse. The characters Jim and Pam proceed to visit the farm, where they choose the "irrigation" themed room. They choose to participate in various farm activities, ncluding plowing the fields, making wine from beets, and watching a table making demonstration. In the episode, Dwight explains that Trip Advisor is the lifeblood of the agritourism industry. The episode portrayed agritourism in a somewhat unappealing light, as Dwight's beet farm and rural lifestyle are often objects of ridicule on the show. Still, the episode brought the concept of agritourism to the show's many viewers.

Dude Ranches

Dude (or guest) ranches offer tourists the chance to work on cattle ranches, and sometimes participate in cattle drives. The fact sheet, *Promoting the Farm and Ranch Recreation Business*, gives farmers and ranchers information on marketing and developing strategies to win tourism dollars. Dude ranches are common in the United States and Australian Outback.

Culinary Tourism

Judging by the surge since 2001 in the number of times "culinary tourism" has appeared as a subject matter or in a session title in tourism industry conferences and programs, we can see that Culinary Tourism is valued by tourism industry professionals as one of the most popular niches in the world's tourism industry. This makes sense, given recent consumer focus on healthy and organic eating, culinary/food pedigrees, and the simple fact that all travellers must eat. Not every visitor goes shopping or visits museums, but all travellers eat. For anyone who doubts, look at the increase in cooking shows featured on The Travel Channel [Anthony Bourdain No Reservations] or travel shows featured on The Food Network [Rachel Ray's $40 a Day series], as examples.

Culinary Tourism is not just experiences of the highest caliber - that would be gourmet tourism. This is perhaps best illustrated by the notion that Culinary Tourism is about what is "unique and memorable, not what is necessarily pretentious and exclusive". Similarly, wine tourism, beer tourism and spa tourism are also regarded as subsets of culinary tourism.

Cultural Tourism

'Cultural tourism' (or culture tourism) is the subset of tourism concerned with a country or region's culture, specifically the lifestyle of the people in those geographical areas, the history of those peoples, their art, architecture, religion(s), and other elements that helped shape their way of life. Cultural tourism includes tourism in urban areas, particularly historic or large cities and their cultural facilities such as museums and theatres. It can also include tourism in rural areas showcasing the traditions of indigenous cultural communities (i.e. festivals, rituals), and their values and lifestyle.

It is generally agreed that cultural tourists spend substantially more than standard tourists do. This form of tourism is also becoming generally more popular throughout the world, and a recent OECD report has highlighted the role that cultural tourism can play in regional development in different world regions. Cultural tourism has been defined as 'the movement of persons to cultural attractions away from their normal place of residence, with the intention to gather new information and experiences to satisfy their cultural needs'.

Destinations

One type of cultural tourism destination is living cultural areas. For an indigenous culture that has stayed largely separated from the surrounding majority, tourism can present both advantages and problems. On the positive side are the unique cultural practices and arts that attract the curiosity of tourists and provide opportunities for tourism and economic development. On the negative side is the issue of how to control tourism so that those same cultural amenities are not destroyed and the people do not feel violated. Other destinations include historical sites, modern urban districts, theme parks and country clubs, coastal or island ecosystems, and inland natural areas.

Key Principles

Destination Planning

As the issue of globalization takes place to this modern time, the challenge of preserving the few remaining cultural community around the world is becoming hard. In a tribal based community, reaching economic advancement with minimal negative impacts is an essential objective to any destination planner. Since they are using the culture of the region as the main attraction, sustainable destination development of the area is vital for them to prevent the negative impacts (i.e. destroying the authentic identity of the tribal community) due to tourism.

Management Issues

Certainly, the principle of "one size fits all" doesn't apply to destination planning. The needs, expectations, and anticipated benefits from tourism vary greatly from one destination to another. This is clearly exemplified as local communities living in regions with tourism potential (destinations) develop a vision for what kind of tourism they want to facilitate, depending on issues and concerns they want to be settled or satisfied.

Destination Planning Resources

Planning Guides

Culture: the heart of development policy: It is important that the destination planner takes into account the diverse definition of culture as the term is subjective. Satisfying tourists' interests such as landscapes, seascapes, art, nature, traditions, ways of life and other products associated to them -which may be categorized cultural in the broadest sense of the word, is a prime consideration as it marks the initial phase of the development of a cultural destination.

The quality of service and destination, which doesn't solely depend on the cultural heritage but more importantly to the cultural environment, can further be developed by setting controls and policies which shall govern the community and its stakeholders. It is therefore safe to say that the planner should be on the ball with the varying meaning of culture itself as this fuels the formulation of development policies that shall entail efficient planning and monitored growth.

Local community, tourists, the destination and sustainable tourism: While satisfying tourists' interests and demands may be a top priority, it is also imperative to ruminate the subsystems of the destination's *(residents)*. Development pressures should be anticipated and set to their minimum level so as to conserve the area's resources and prevent a saturation of the destination as to not abuse the product and the residents correspondingly. The plan should incorporate the locals to its gain by training and employing them and in the process encourage them to participate to the travel business. Keep in mind that the plan should make travellers not only aware about the destination but also concern on how to help it sustain its character while broadening their travelling experience.

Planning Tools

Sources of Data

The core of a planner's job is to design an appropriate planning process and facilitate community decision. Ample information which is a crucial requirement is contributed through various technical researches and analyzes. Here are some of the helpful tools commonly used by planners to aid them:

1. Key Informant Interviews
2. Libraries, Internet, and Survey Research
3. Census and Statistical Analysis
4. Spatial Analysis with Geographical Information System (GIS) and Global Positioning System (GPS) technologies

Key Institutions

Participating structures are primarily led by the government's local authorities and the official tourism board or council, with the involvement of various NGOs, community and indigenous representatives, development organizations, and the academe.

Case Studies: Mountainous Regions of Central Asia and in the Himalayas

Tourism is coming to the previously isolated but spectacular mountainous regions of Central Asia, the Hindu Kush and the Himalayas. Closed for so many years to visitors from abroad, it now attracts a growing number of foreign tourists by its unique culture and splendid natural beauty. However, while this influx of tourists is bringing economic opportunities and employment to local populations, helping to promote these little-known regions of the world, it has also brought challenges along with it: to ensure that it is well-managed and that its benefits are shared by all.

As a response to this concern, the Norwegian Government, as well as the UNESCO, organized an interdisciplinary project called the Development of Cultural and Ecotourism in the Mountainous Regions of Central Asia and the Himalayas project. It aims to establish links and promote cooperation between local communities, national and international NGOs, and tour agencies in order to heighten the role of the local community and involve them fully in the employment opportunities and income-generating activities that tourism can bring. Project activities include training local tour guides, producing high-quality craft items and promoting home-stays and bed-and-breakfast type accommodation. As of now, the project is drawing on the expertise of international NGOs and tourism professionals in the seven participating countries, making a practical and positive contribution to alleviating poverty by helping local communities to draw the maximum benefit from their region's tourism potential, while protecting the environmental and cultural heritage of the region concerned.

The University of Travelhost, Dallas, Texas has an extensive travel library continually gathering travel related research and tourism economic impact studies nationwide.

Ecotourism

'Ecotourism' (also known as ecological tourism) is responsible travel to fragile, pristine, and usually protected areas that strives to be low impact and (often) small scale. It purports to educate the traveler; provide funds for conservation; directly benefit the economic development and political empowerment of local communities; and foster respect for different cultures and for human rights. Eco tourism is held as important by those who participate in it so that future generations may experience aspects of the environment relatively untouched by human intervention. Most serious studies of ecotourism including several university programs now use this as the working definition.

Ecotourism appeals to ecologically and socially conscious individuals. Generally speaking, it focuses on volunteering, personal growth and environmental responsibility. It typically involves travel to destinations where flora, fauna, and cultural heritage are the primary attractions. One of the goals of ecotourism is to offer tourists insight into the impact of human beings on the environment, and to foster a greater appreciation of our natural habitats.

Responsible ecotourism includes programs that minimize the negative aspects of conventional tourism on the environment and enhance the cultural integrity of local people. Therefore, in addition to evaluating environmental and cultural factors, an integral part of ecotourism is the promotion of recycling, energy efficiency, water conservation, and creation of economic opportunities for local communities.

Criteria

Ecotourism is a form of tourism that involves travelling to tranquil and unpolluted natural areas. According to the definition and principles of ecotourism established by The International Ecotourism Society (TIES) in 1990, ecotourism is "Responsible travel to natural areas that conserves the environment and improves the well-being of local people." (TIES, 1990). Martha Honey, expands on the TIES definition by describing the seven characteristics of ecotourism, which are:

- Involves travel to natural destinations.
- Minimizes impact.
- Builds environmental awareness.
- Provides direct financial benefits for conservation.
- Provides financial benefits and empowerment for local people.
- Respects local culture.
- Supports human rights and democratic movements.

Ideally, ecotourism should satisfy several criteria, such as:

- conservation of biological diversity and cultural diversity through ecosystem protection
- promotion of sustainable use of biodiversity, by providing jobs to local populations
- sharing of socioeconomic benefits with local communities and indigenous peoples by having their informed consent and participation in the management of ecotourism enterprises
- tourism to unspoiled natural resources, with minimal impact on the environment being a primary concern.
- minimization of tourism's own environmental impact
- affordability and lack of waste in the form of luxury
- local culture, flora and fauna being the main attractions

For many countries, ecotourism is not simply a marginal activity to finance protection of the environment, but is a major industry of the national economy. For example, in Costa Rica, Ecuador, Nepal, Kenya, Madagascar and Antarctica, ecotourism represents a significant portion of the gross domestic product and economic activity.

The concept of ecotourism is widely misunderstood and in practice is often used as a marketing tool to promote tourism that is related to nature. This is an especially frequent malpractice in the realm of Jungle tourism. Critics claim that these greenwashing practices, carried out in the name of ecotourism, often consist of placing a hotel in a splendid landscape, to the detriment of the ecosystem.

According to them, ecotourism must above all sensitize people to the beauty and the fragility of nature. They condemn some operators as greenwashing their operations: using the labels of "green" and "eco-friendly", while behaving in environmentally irresponsible ways. Although academics disagree about who can be classified as an ecotourist and there is little statistical data, some estimate that more than five million ecotourists - the majority of the ecotourist population - come from the United States, with many others from Western Europe, Canada and Australia.

Currently, there are various moves to create national and international ecotourism accreditation programs, although the process is also controversial. National ecotourism certification programs have been put in place in countries such as Costa Rica, Australia, Kenya and Sweden.

History

Ecotourism, responsible tourism, jungle tourism, and sustainable development have become prevalent concepts since the late 1980s, and ecotourism has experienced arguably the fastest growth of all sub-sectors in the tourism industry. The popularity represents a change in tourist perceptions, increased environmental awareness, and a desire to explore natural environments. At times, such changes become as much a statement affirming one's social identity, educational sophistication, and disposable income as it has about preserving the Amazon rainforest or the Caribbean reef for posterity.

Criticisms

Definitional Problems and Greenwashing

To approach an understanding of the problem, a clear definition must delineate what is, and is not, ecotourism. Ideally, ecotourism satisfies several general criteria, including the conservation of biological diversity and cultural diversity through ecosystem protection, promotion of sustainable use of biodiversity, share of social-economic benefits with local communities through informed consent and participation, increase in environmental and cultural knowledge, affordability and reduced waste, and minimization of its own environmental impact.

In such ways, it contributes to the long term benefits to both the environment and local communities.

However, in the continuum of tourism activities that stretch from conventional tourism to ecotourism proper, there has been a lot of contention to the limit at which biodiversity preservation, local social-economic benefits, and environmental impact can be considered "ecotourism".

For this reason, environmentalists, special interest groups, and governments define ecotourism differently. Environmental organizations have generally insisted that ecotourism is nature-based, sustainably managed, conservation supporting, and environmentally educated. The tourist industry and governments, however, focus more on the product aspect, treating ecotourism as equivalent to any sort of tourism based in nature. As a further complication, many terms are used under the rubric of ecotourism. Nature tourism, low impact tourism, green tourism, bio-tourism, ecologically responsible tourism, and others have been used in literature and marketing, although they are not necessary synonymous with ecotourism.

The problems associated with defining ecotourism have led to confusion among tourists and academics alike. Definitional problems are also subject of considerable public controversy and concern because of green washing, a trend towards the commercialization of tourism schemes disguised as sustainable, nature based, and environmentally friendly ecotourism. According to McLaren, these schemes are environmentally destructive, economically exploitative, and culturally insensitive at its worst. They are also morally disconcerting because they mislead tourists and manipulate their concerns for the environment.

Despite objections, green washing continues to grow unabated. The Nature's Sacred Paradise, a theme park in Quintana Roo, Mexico, is responsible for displacing local Mayan communities and illegally keeping endangered species in captivity to attract visitors. The development and success of such large scale, energy intensive, and ecologically unsustainable schemes are a testament to the tremendous profits associated with being labeled as ecotourism.

Negative Impact of Tourism

Ecotourism has become one of the fastest-growing sectors of the tourism industry, growing annually by 10-15% worldwide (Miller, 2007). One definition of ecotourism is "the practice of low-impact, educational, ecologically and culturally sensitive travel that benefits local communities and host countries" (Honey, 1999). Many of the ecotourism projects are not meeting these standards. Even if some of the guidelines are being executed, the local communities are still facing other negative impacts.

South Africa is one of the countries that are reaping significant economic benefits from ecotourism, but negative effects - including forcing people to leave their homes, gross violations of fundamental rights, and environmental hazards - far outweigh the medium-term economic benefits (Miller, 2007).

A tremendous amount of money is being spent and human resources continue to be used for ecotourism despite unsuccessful outcomes, and even more money is put into public relation campaigns to dilute the effects of criticism. Ecotourism channels resources away from other projects that could contribute more sustainable and realistic solutions to pressing social and environmental problems. "The money tourism can generate often ties parks and managements to eco-tourism" (Walpole et al. 2001). But there is a tension in this relationship because eco-tourism often causes conflict and changes in land-use rights, fails to deliver promises of community-level benefits, damages environments, and has plenty of other social impacts.

Indeed many argue repeatedly that eco-tourism is neither ecologically nor socially beneficial, yet it persists as a strategy for conservation and development (West, 2006). While several studies are being done on ways to improve the ecotourism structure, some argue that these examples provide rationale for stopping it altogether.

The ecotourism system exercises tremendous financial and political influence. The evidence above shows that a strong case exists for restraining such activities in certain locations. Funding could be used for field studies aimed at finding alternative solutions to tourism and the diverse problems Africa faces in result of urbanization, industrialization, and the over exploitation of agriculture (Kamuaro, 2007).

At the local level, ecotourism has become a source of conflict over control of land, resources, and tourism profits. In this case, ecotourism has harmed the environment and local people, and has led to conflicts over profit distribution. In a perfect world more efforts would be made towards educating tourists of the environmental and social effects of their travels. Very few regulations or laws stand in place as boundaries for the investors in ecotourism. These should be implemented to prohibit the promotion of unsustainable ecotourism projects and materials which project false images of destinations, demeaning local and indigenous cultures.

Direct Environmental Impacts

Ecotourism operations occasionally fail to live up to conservation ideals. It is sometimes overlooked that ecotourism is a highly consumer-centred activity, and that environmental conservation is a means to further economic growth.

Although ecotourism is intended for small groups, even a modest increase in population, however temporary, puts extra pressure on the local environment and necessitates the development of additional infrastructure and amenities. The construction of water treatment plants, sanitation facilities, and lodges come with the exploitation of non-renewable energy sources and the utilization of already limited local resources.

The conversion of natural land to such tourist infrastructure is implicated in deforestation and habitat deterioration of butterflies in Mexico and squirrel monkeys in Costa Rica. In other cases, the environment suffers because local communities are unable to meet the infrastructure demands of ecotourism. The lack of adequate sanitation facilities in many East African parks results in the disposal of campsite sewage in rivers, contaminating the wildlife, livestock, and people who draw drinking water from it.

Aside from environmental degradation with tourist infrastructure, population pressures from ecotourism also leaves behind garbage and pollution associated with the Western lifestyle. Although ecotourists claim to be educationally sophisticated and environmentally concerned, they rarely understand the ecological consequences of their visits and how their day-to-day activities append physical impacts on the environment.

As one scientist observes, they "rarely acknowledge how the meals they eat, the toilets they flush, the water they drink, and so on, are all part of broader regional economic and ecological systems they are helping to reconfigure with their very activities." Nor do ecotourists recognize the great consumption of non-renewable energy required to arrive at their destination, which is typically more remote than conventional tourism destinations. For instance, an exotic journey to a place 10,000 kilometers away consumes about 700 litres of fuel per person.

Ecotourism activities are, in of itself, issues in environmental impact because they disturb fauna and flora. Ecotourists believe that because they are only taking pictures and leaving footprints, they keep ecotourism sites pristine, but even harmless sounding activities such as a nature hike can be ecologically destructive. In the Annapurna Circuit in Nepal, ecotourists have worn down the marked trails and created alternate routes, contributing to soil impaction, erosion, and plant damage. Where the ecotourism activity involves wildlife viewing, it can scare away animals, disrupt their feeding and nesting sites, or acclimate them to the presence of people. In Kenya, wildlife-observer disruption drives cheetahs off their reserves, increasing the risk of inbreeding and further endangering the species.

Environmental Hazards

Unfortunately, industrialization, urbanization, and unsustainable agriculture practices have all had serious effects on the environment. Ecotourism is now also playing a role in this depletion. While the term ecotourism may sound relatively benign, one of its most serious impacts is its consumption of virgin territories (Kamuaro, 2007). These invasions often include deforestation, disruption of ecological life systems and various forms of pollution, all of which contribute to environmental degradation. The number of motor vehicles crossing the park increases as tour drivers search for rare species.

The number of roads has disrupted the grass cover which has serious effects on plant and animal species. These areas also have a higher rate of disturbances and invasive species because of all the traffic moving off the beaten path into new undiscovered areas (Kamuaro, 2007).

Ecotourism also has an effect on species through the value placed on them. "Certain species have gone from being little known or valued by local people to being highly valued commodities. The commodification of plants may erase their social value and lead to overproduction within protected areas. Local people and their images can also be turned into commodities" (West, 2006). Kamuaro brings up a relatively obvious contradiction, any commercial venture into unspoiled, pristine land with or without the "eco" prefix as a contradiction in terms. To generate revenue you have to have a high number of traffic, tourists, which inevitably means a higher pressure on the environment.

Local People

Most forms of ecotourism are owned by foreign investors and corporations that provide few benefits to local communities. An overwhelming majority of profits are put into the pockets of investors instead of reinvestment into the local economy or environmental protection. The limited numbers of local people who are employed in the economy enter at its lowest level, and are unable to live in tourist areas because of meager wages and a two market system.

In some cases, the resentment by local people results in environmental degradation. As a highly publicized case, the Masai nomads in Kenya killed wildlife in national parks to show aversion to unfair compensation terms and displacement from traditional lands. The lack of economic opportunities for local people also constrains them to degrade the environment as a means of sustenance. The presence of affluent ecotourists encourage the development of destructive markets in wildlife souvenirs, such as the sale of coral trinkets on tropical islands and animal products in Asia, contributing to illegal harvesting and poaching from the environment. In Suriname, sea turtle reserves use a large portion of their budget to guard against these destructive activities.

Displacement of People

One of the most powerful examples of communities being moved in order to create a park is the story of the Masai. About 70% of national parks and game reserves in East Africa are on Masai land (Kamuaro, 2007). The first undesirable impact of tourism was that of the extent of land lost from the Masai culture. Local and national governments took advantage of the Masai's ignorance on the situation and robbed them of huge chunks of grazing land, putting to risk their only socioeconomic livelihood. In Kenya the Masai also have not gained any economic benefits. Despite the loss of their land, employment favours better educated workers. Furthermore the investors in this area are not local and have not put profits back into local economy. In some cases game reserves can be created without informing or consulting local people, who come to find out about the situation when an eviction notice is delivered (Kamuaro, 2007). Another source of resentment is the manipulation of the local people by their government. "Eco-tourism works to create simplistic images of local people and their uses and understandings of their surroundings. Through the lens of these simplified images, officials direct policies and projects towards the local people and the local people are blamed if the projects fail" (West, 2006). Clearly tourism as a trade is not empowering the local people who make it rich and satisfying. Instead ecotourism exploits and depletes, particularly in African Masai tribes. It has to be reoriented if it is to be useful to local communities and to become sustainable (Kamuaro, 2007).

Threats to Indigenous Cultures

Ecotourism often claims that it preserves and "enhances" local cultures. However, evidence shows that with the establishment of protected areas local people have illegally lost their homes, and most often with no compensation (Kamuaro, 2007). Pushing people onto marginal lands with harsh climates, poor soils, lack of water, and infested with livestock and disease does little to enhance livelihoods even when a proportion of ecotourism profits are directed back into the community. The establishment of parks can create harsh survival realities and deprive the people of their traditional use of land and natural resources. Ethnic groups are increasingly being seen as a "backdrop" to the scenery and wildlife. The local people struggle for cultural survival and freedom of cultural expression while being "observed" by tourists. Local indigenous people also have strong resentment towards the change, "Tourism has been allowed to develop with virtually no controls. Too many lodges have been built, too much firewood is being used and no limits are being placed on tourism vehicles. They regularly drive off-track and harass the wildlife. Their vehicle tracks crisscross the entire Masai Mara. Inevitably the bush is becoming eroded and degraded" (Kamuaro, 2007).

Mismanagement

While governments are typically entrusted with the administration and enforcement of environmental protection, they often lack the commitment or capability to manage ecotourism sites effectively. The regulations for environmental protection may be vaguely defined, costly to implement, hard to enforce, and uncertain in effectiveness. Government regulatory agencies, as political bodies, are susceptible to making decisions that spend budget on politically beneficial but environmentally unproductive projects. Because of prestige and conspicuousness, the construction of an attractive visitor's centre at an ecotourism site may take precedence over more pressing environmental concerns like acquiring habitat, protecting endemic species, and removing invasive ones. Finally, influential groups can pressure and sway the interests of the government to their favour. The government and its regulators can become vested in the benefits of the ecotourism industry which they are supposed to regulate, causing restrictive environmental regulations and enforcement to become more lenient.

Management of ecotourism sites by private ecotourism companies offers an alternative to the cost of regulation and deficiency of government agencies. It is believed that these companies have a self interest in limited environmental degradation, because tourists will pay more for pristine environments, which translates to higher profit. However, theory indicates that this practice is not economically feasible and will fail to manage the environment.

The model of monopolistic competition states that distinctiveness will entail profits, but profits will promote imitation. A company that protects its ecotourism sites is able to charge a premium for the novel experience and pristine environment. But when other companies view the success of this approach, they also enter the market with similar practices, increasing competition and reducing demand. Eventually, the demand will be reduced until the economic profit is zero. A cost-benefit analysis shows that the company bears the cost of environmental protection without receiving the gains. Without economic incentive, the whole premise of self interest through environmental protection is quashed; instead, ecotourism companies will minimize environment related expenses and maximize tourism demand.

The tragedy of the commons offers another model for economic unsustainability from environmental protection, in ecotourism sites utilized by many companies. Although there is a communal incentive to protect the environment, maximizing the benefits in the long run, a company will conclude that it is in their best interest to utilize the ecotourism site beyond its sustainable level. By increasing the number of ecotourists, for instance, a company gains all the economic benefit while paying only a part of the environmental cost. In the same way, a company recognizes that there is no incentive to actively protect the environment; they bear all the costs, while the benefits are shared by all other companies. The result, again, is mismanagement.

Taken together, the mobility of foreign investment and lack of economic incentive for environmental protection means that ecotourism companies are disposed to establishing themselves in new sites once their existing one is sufficiently degraded.

Improving Sustainability

Regulation and Accreditation

Because the regulation of ecotourism is poorly implemented or nonexistent, ecologically destructive greenwashed operations like underwater hotels, helicopter tours, and wildlife theme parks are categorized as ecotourism along with canoeing, camping, photography, and wildlife observation. The failure to acknowledge responsible, low impact ecotourism puts these companies at a competitive disadvantage.

Many environmentalists have argued for a global standard of accreditation, differentiating ecotourism companies based on their level of environmental commitment. A national or international regulatory board would enforce accreditation procedures, with representation from various groups including governments, hotels, tour operators, travel agents, guides, airlines, local authorities, conservation organizations, and non-governmental organizations. The decisions of the board would be sanctioned by governments, so that non-compliant companies would be legally required to disassociate themselves from the use of the ecotourism brand.

Crinion suggests a Green Stars System, based on criteria including a management plan, benefit for the local community, small group interaction, education value and staff training. Ecotourists who consider their choices would be confident of a genuine ecotourism experience when they see the higher star rating. In addition, environmental impact assessments could be used as a form of accreditation. Feasibility is evaluated from a scientific basis, and recommendations could be made to optimally plan infrastructure, set tourist capacity, and manage the ecology. This form of accreditation is more sensitive to site specific conditions.

Guidelines and Education

An environmental protection strategy must address the issue of ecotourists removed from the cause-and-effect of their actions on the environment. More initiatives should be carried out to improve their awareness, sensitize them to environmental issues, and care about the places they visit.

Tour guides are an obvious and direct medium to communicate awareness. With the confidence of ecotourists and intimate knowledge of the environment, they can actively discuss conservation issues. A tour guide training program in Costa Rica's Tortuguero National Park has helped mitigate negative environmental impacts by providing information and regulating tourists on the parks' beaches used by nesting endangered sea turtles.

Small Scale, Slow Growth and Local Control

The underdevelopment theory of tourism describes a new form of imperialism by multinational corporations that control ecotourism resources. These corporations finance and profit from the development of large scale ecotourism that causes excessive environmental degradation, loss of traditional culture and way of life, and exploitation of local labour. In Zimbabwe and Nepal's Annapurna region, where underdevelopment is taking place, more than 90 percent of ecotourism revenues are expatriated to the parent countries, and less than 5 percent go into local communities.

The lack of sustainability highlights the need for small scale, slow growth, and locally based ecotourism. Local peoples have a vested interest in the well being of their community, and are therefore more accountable to environmental protection than multinational corporations. The lack of control, westernization, adverse impacts to the environment, loss of culture and traditions outweigh the benefits of establishing large scale ecotourism.

The increased contributions of communities to locally managed ecotourism create viable economic opportunities, including high level management positions, and reduce environmental issues associated with poverty and unemployment. Because the ecotourism experience is marketed to a different lifestyle from large scale ecotourism, the development of facilities and infrastructure does not need to conform to corporate Western tourism standards, and can be much simpler and less expensive. There is a greater multiplier effect on the economy, because local products, materials, and labour are used. Profits accrue locally and import leakages are reduced.

However, even this form of tourism may require foreign investment for promotion or start up. When such investments are required, it is crucial for communities for find a company or non-governmental organization that reflects the philosophy of ecotourism; sensitive to their concerns and willing to cooperate at the expense of profit. The basic assumption of the multiplier effect is that the economy starts off with unused resources, for example, that many workers are cyclically unemployed and much of industrial capacity is sitting idle or incompletely utilized. By increasing demand in the economy it is then possible to boost production. If the economy was already at full employment, with only structural, frictional, or other supply-side types of unemployment, any attempt to boost demand would only lead to inflation. For various laissez-faire schools of economics which embrace Say's Law and deny the possibility of Keynesian inefficiency and under-employment of resources, therefore, the multiplier concept is irrelevant or wrong-headed.

As an example, consider the government increasing its expenditure on roads by $one million, without a corresponding increase in taxation. This sum would go to the road builders, who would hire more workers and distribute the money as wages and profits. The households receiving these incomes will save part of the money and spend the rest on consumer goods. These expenditures in turn will generate more jobs, wages, and profits, and so on with the income and spending circulating around the economy.

The multiplier effect arises because of the induced increases in consumer spending which occur due to the increased incomes — and because of the feedback into increasing business revenues, jobs, and income again. This process does not lead to an economic explosion not only because of the supply-side barriers at potential output (full employment) but because at each "round", the increase in consumer spending is less than the increase in consumer incomes. That is, the marginal propensity to consume (mpc) is less than one, so that each round some extra income goes into saving, leaking out of the cumulative process. Each increase in spending is thus smaller than that of the previous round, preventing an explosion. Ecotourism has to be implemented with care.

Natural Resource Management

Natural resource management can be utilized as a specialized tool for the development of eco-tourism. There are several places throughout the world where the amount of natural resources are abundant. But, with human encroachment and habitats these resources are depleting. Without knowing the proper utilization of certain resources they are destroyed and floral and faunal species are becoming extinct. Ecotourism programmes can be introduced for the conservation of these resources. Several plans and proper management programmes can be introduced so that these resources remain untouched. Several organizations, NGO's, scientists are working on this field.

Natural resources of hill areas like Kurseong in West Bengal are plenty in number with various flora and fauna, but tourism for business purpose poised the situation. Researcher from Jadavpur University presently working in this area for the development of eco-tourism which can be utilized as a tool for natural resource management.

In South-East Asia government and Non-Government Organisations are working together with academics and industry operators to spread the economic benefits of tourism into the kampungs and villages of the region. A recently formed alliance, the South-East Asian Tourism Organisation - SEATO is bringing together these diverse players to allay resource management concerns.

Tour Operators, Travel Agencies & Retailers

Some companies specialise in ecotourism, designing their trips to be environmentally, culturally and socially friendly. Companies such as Intrepid Travel, Adventure Life, Frontier, and Marine Conservation Society, Family Nature Summit, Peregrine Adventures, World Expeditions, greentraveller, Explore Worldwide and Exodus offer trips catering for the thoughtful traveller. Some tour operators are keenly aware of the impacts that they may have on specific areas and rotate clients around to different sites for snorkeling, bird watching, and other activities. Others are just beginning to see the advantage of "green" travel destinations.

Extreme Tourism

Extreme tourism or shock tourism is a type of niche tourism involving travel to dangerous places (mountains, jungles, deserts, caves, etc.) or participation in dangerous events. Extreme tourism overlaps with extreme sport. The two share the main attraction, "adrenaline rush" caused by an element of risk, and differing mostly in the degree of engagement and professionalism.

Extreme tourism is a growing business in the countries of the former Soviet Union (Russia, Ukraine, Azerbaijan, etc.) and in South American countries like Peru, Chile and Argentina. The mountainous and rugged terrain of Northern Pakistan has also developed into a popular extreme tourism location.

While traditional tourism requires significant investments in hotels, roads, etc., extreme tourism requires much less to jump-start a business. In addition to traditional travel-based tourism destinations, various exotic attractions are suggested, such as flyovers in MiGs at Mach 2.5, ice diving in the White Sea, or travelling across the Chernobyl zone.

Geotourism

Geotourism is "best practice" tourism that sustains, or even enhances, the geographical character of a place, such as its culture, environment, heritage, and the well-being of its residents.

The concept was introduced publicly in a 2002 report by the Travel Industry Association of America (as of 2009 this organization adapted name to U.S. Travel Association) and National Geographic Traveler magazine. National Geographic senior editor Jonathan B. Tourtellot and his wife, Sally Bensusen, coined the term in 1997 in response to requests for a term and concept more encompassing than *ecotourism* and *sustainable tourism*.

Like ecotourism, geotourism promotes a virtuous circle whereby tourism revenues provide a local incentive to protect what tourists are coming to see, but extends the principle beyond nature and ecology to incorporate all characteristics that contribute to *sense of place*, such as historic structures, living and traditional culture, landscapes, cuisine, arts and artisanry, as well as local flora and fauna. Geotourism incorporates sustainability principles, but in addition to the do-no-harm ethic, geotourism focuses on the place as a whole. The idea of enhancement allows for development based on character of place, rather than standardized international branding, and generic architecture, food, and so on.

The Geotourism Charter

The National Geographic Society defines geoturism as tourism that sustains or enhances the geographical character of a place – its environment, culture, aesthetics, heritage, and the well-being of its residents.

National Geographic Society has also drawn up a "Geotourism Charter" based on 13 principles:

1. *Integrity of place:* Enhance geographical character by developing and improving it in ways distinctive to the local, reflective of its natural and cultural heritage, so as to encourage market differentiation and cultural pride.
2. *International codes:* Adhere to the principles embodied in the World Tourism Organization's Global Code of Ethics for Tourism and the Principles of the Cultural Tourism Charter established by the International Council on Monuments and Sites (ICOMOS).

3. *Market selectivity:* Encourage growth in tourism market segments most likely to appreciate, respect, and disseminate information about the distinctive assets of the locale.
4. *Market diversity:* Encourage a full range of appropriate food and lodging facilities, so as to appeal to the entire demographic spectrum of the geotourism market and so maximize economic resiliency over both the short and long term.
5. *Tourist satisfaction:* Ensure that satisfied, excited geotourists bring new vacation stories home and send friends off to experience the same thing, thus providing continuing demand for the destination.
6. *Community involvement:* Base tourism on community resources to the extent possible, encouraging local small businesses and civic groups to build partnerships to promote and provide a distinctive, honest visitor experience and market their locales effectively. Help businesses develop approaches to tourism that build on the area's nature, history and culture, including food and drink, artisanry, performance arts, etc.
7. *Community benefit:* Encourage micro- to medium-size enterprises and tourism business strategies that emphasize economic and social benefits to involved communities, especially poverty alleviation, with clear communication of the destination stewardship policies required to maintain those benefits.
8. *Protection and enhancement of destination appeal:* Encourage businesses to sustain natural habitats, heritage sites, aesthetic appeal, and local culture. Prevent degradation by keeping volumes of tourists within maximum acceptable limits. Seek business models that can operate profitably within those limits. Use persuasion, incentives, and legal enforcement as needed.
9. *Land use:* Anticipate development pressures and apply techniques to prevent undesired overdevelopment and

degradation. Contain resort and vacation-home sprawl, especially on coasts and islands, so as to retain a diversity of natural and scenic environments and ensure continued resident access to waterfronts. Encourage major self-contained tourism attractions, such as large-scale theme parks and convention centres unrelated to character of place, to be sited in needier locations with no significant ecological, scenic, or cultural assets.

10. *Conservation of resources:* Encourage businesses to minimize water pollution, solid waste, energy consumption, water usage, landscaping chemicals, and overly bright nighttime lighting. Advertise these measures in a way that attracts the large, environmentally sympathetic tourist market.
11. *Planning:* Recognize and respect immediate economic needs without sacrificing long-term character and the geotourism potential of the destination. Where tourism attracts in-migration of workers, develop new communities that themselves constitute a destination enhancement. Strive to diversify the economy and limit population influx to sustainable levels. Adopt public strategies for mitigating practices that are incompatible with geotourism and damaging to the image of the destination.
12. *Interactive interpretation:* Engage both visitors and hosts in learning about the place. Encourage residents to show off the natural and cultural heritage of their communities, so that tourists gain a richer experience and residents develop pride in their locales.
13. *Evaluation:* Establish an evaluation process to be conducted on a regular basis by an independent panel representing all stakeholder interests, and publicize evaluation results.

Heritage Tourism

Cultural heritage tourism (or just heritage tourism) is a branch of tourism oriented towards the cultural heritage of the location where tourism is occurring.

Culture has always been a major object of travel, as the development of the Grand Tour from the 16th century onwards attests. In the 20th century, some people have claimed, culture ceased to be the objective of tourism: tourism is now culture. Cultural attractions play an important role in tourism at all levels, from the global highlights of world culture to attractions that underpin local identities. (Richards, 1996)

According to the Weiler and Hall, culture, heritage and the arts have long contributed to appeal of tourist destination. However, in recent years 'culture' has been rediscovered as an important marketing too! to attract those travellers with special interests in heritage and arts. According to the Hollinshead, cultural heritage tourism defines as cultural heritage tourism is the fastest growing segment of the tourism industry because there is a trend toward an increase specialization among tourists. This trend is evident in the rise in the volume of tourists who seek adventure, culture, history, archaeology and interaction with local people.

Cultural heritage tourism is important for various reasons; it has a positive economic and social impact, it establishes and reinforces identity, it helps preserve the cultural heritage, with culture as an instrument it facilitates harmony and understanding among people, it supports culture and helps renew tourism (Richards, 1996). Putangina Cultural heritage tourism has a number of objectives that must be met within the context of sustainable development such as; the conservation of cultural resources, accurate interpretation of resources, authentic visitors experience, and the stimulation of the earned revenues of cultural resources. We can see, therefore, that cultural heritage tourism is not only concerned with identification, management and protection of the heritage values but it must also be involved in understanding the impact of tourism on communities and regions, achieving economic and social benefits, providing financial resources for protection, as well as marketing and promotion. (J. M. Fladmark, 1994)

Heritage tourism involves visiting historical or industrial sites that may include old canals, railways, battlegrounds, etc. The overall purpose is to gain an appreciation of the past. It also refers to the marketing of a location to members of a diaspora who have distant family roots there. Decolonization and immigration form the major background of múch contemporary heritage tourism.

Falling travel costs have also made heritage tourism possible for more people.

Another possible form involves religious travel or pilgrimages. Many Catholics from around the world come to the Vatican and other sites such as Lourdes or Fátima. Large numbers of Jews have both visited Israel and emigrated there. Many have also gone to Holocaust sites and memorials. Islam commands its followers to take the *hajj* to Mecca, thus differentiating it somewhat from tourism in the usual sense, though the trip can also be a culturally important event for the pilgrim.

Heritage Tourism can also be attributed to historical events that have been dramatised to make them more entertaining. For example a historical tour of a town or city using a theme such as ghosts or vikings.

LGBT Tourism

Gay tourism or LGBT tourism is a form of niche tourism marketed to gay, lesbian, bisexual and transgender (LGBT) people. They are usually open about their sexual orientation and gender identity but may be more or less open when travelling; for instance they may be closeted at home or if they have come out, may be more discreet in areas known for violence against LGBT people. The main components of LGBT tourism is for cities and countries wishing to attract LGBT tourists; people looking to travel to LGBT-friendly destinations; people wanting travel with other LGBT people when travelling regardless of the destination and LGBT travellers who are mainly concerned with cultural and safety issues. The slang term *gaycation* has come to imply a version of a vacation that includes a pronounced aspect of LGBT culture, either in the journey or destination. The LGBT tourism industry includes travel agents, tour companies, cruise lines and travel advertising and promotions companies who market these destinations to the gay community. Coinciding with the increased visibility of LGBT people raising children in the 1990s, an increase in family-friendly LGBT tourism has emerged in the 2000s, for instance R Family Vacations which includes activities and entertainment geared towards couples including same-sex weddings. R Family's first cruise was held aboard Norwegian Cruise Lines's *Norwegian Dawn* with 1600 passengers including 600 children.

Major companies in the travel industry have become aware of the substantial money (also known as the "pink dollar" or "pink pound") generated by this marketing niche, and have made it a point to align themselves with the gay community and gay tourism campaigns. According to a 2000 Tourism Intelligence International report 10% of international tourists were gay and lesbian accounting for more than 70 million arrivals worldwide. This market segment is expected to continue to grow as a result ongoing acceptance of LGBT people and changing attitudes towards sexual and gender minorities. The gay and lesbian segment is estimated at $55 billion annual market as of 2007. Outside larger companies, LGBT tourists are offered other traditional tourism tools, such as LGBT hospitality networks of LGBT individuals who offer each other hospitality during their travels and even home swaps where people live in each others homes. Also available are social groups for resident and visiting gay, lesbian, bisexual and transgender expatriates and friends exist worldwide.

Gay Travel Destinations

Gay travel destinations are popular among practitioners of gay tourism because they usually have permissive or liberal attitudes towards gays, feature a prominent gay infrastructure (bars, businesses, restaurants, hotels, nightlife, entertainment, media, organisations, etc.), the opportunity to socialize with other gays, and the feeling that one can relax safely among other gay people.

Gay travel destinations are often large cities, although not exclusively, and often coincide with the existence of gay neighborhoods. These municipalities and their tourism bureaus often work actively to develop their reputations as places for gays to travel to, commonly by aligning themselves to local gay organisations. Travel analysts state that the existence of a core gay friendly population is often the primary catalyst for the development of a gay-friendly tourist destination.

Gay tourism might also coincide with special gay events such as annual gay pride parades, gay neighborhood festivals and such gay community gatherings as gay chorus festivals and concerts, gay square dance conventions, gay sports meets such as Gay Games, World Outgames or Euro Games and conferences of national and international gay organisations. Gay tourism blossoms during these peak periods.

Gay tourism practitioners spend $64 billion a year on gay travel, according to Community Marketing Inc. The adult GLBT community has a total economic spending power of more than $600 billion per year, according to Wietck Combs. Philadelphia and Community Marketing found that for every one dollar invested in gay tourism marketing, $153 was returned in direct economic spending in shops, hotels, restaurants and attractions. Since 2002, there has been a historic rise in gay tourism marketing. Destinations such as Philadelphia, Dallas and Ft. Lauderdale have engaged in gay tourism campaigns. The gay cruise industry is experiencing a significant growth period. Community Marketing Inc. found in research studies that gay business travellers are 30% more likely to convert to a leisure visitor.

Philadelphia was the first destination in the world to create and air a television commercial specifically geared towards practitioners of gay tourism. Philadelphia was also the first destination to commission a research study aimed at a specific destination to learn about gay travel to a specific city.

Work is underway in conjunction with Israel's Ministry of Tourism to turn Tel Aviv into the international tourist destination for the gay-lesbian community in order to boost business in restaurants, hotels, city attraction sites and beaches. In an effort to boost gay tourism in Tel Aviv, the Gay and Lesbian Union has bid to host in Tel Aviv the 2009 Euro Pride, the largest annual gay parade in the world.

Gay Tourism Specialists

The International Gay and Lesbian Travel Association (IGLTA) holds an annual world convention and four symposia in different tourism destinations around the world. Each symposium attracts over 100 representatives of tour agencies and travel publications that specialise in the gay and lesbian market. The association was founded in 1983, and it currently represents over 900 members. Its headquarters are in Fort Lauderdale, Florida.

The "14th International Gay & Lesbian World Travel Expo" in 2006 will visit six U.S. cities. The annual Expo series is produced by Community Marketing, a gay tourism research and travel marketing firm.

Out Traveler, from the publishers of *Out* and *The Advocate*, is a glossy magazine aimed at gay and lesbian travellers. It is published six times yearly. Other LGBT-travel publications include Passport Magazine and Spartacus International. One of Europe's gay and lesbian travel marketing specialists is Out Now Consulting.

Medical Tourism

Medical tourism (also called medical travel, health tourism or global healthcare) is a term initially coined by travel agencies and the mass media to describe the rapidly-growing practice of travelling across international borders to obtain health care. It also refers pejoratively to the practice of healthcare providers travelling internationally to deliver healthcare.

Services typically sought by travellers include elective procedures as well as complex specialized surgeries such as joint replacement (knee/hip), cardiac surgery, dental surgery, and cosmetic surgeries. However, virtually every type of health care, including psychiatry, alternative treatments, convalescent care and even burial services are available. As a practical matter, providers and customers commonly use informal channels of communication-connection-contract, and in such cases this tends to mean less regulatory or legal oversight to assure quality and less formal recourse to reimbursement or redress, if needed.

Over 50 countries have identified medical tourism as a national industry. However, accreditation and other measures of quality vary widely across the globe, and there are risks and ethical issues that make this method of accessing medical care controversial. Also, some destinations may become hazardous or even dangerous for medical tourists to contemplate. In the context of global health, "medical tourism" is a pejorative because during such trips health care providers often practice outside of their areas of expertise or hold different (i.e., lower) standards of care. Greater numbers than ever before of student volunteers, health professions trainees, and researchers from resource-rich countries are working temporarily and anticipating future work in resource-starved areas. This emphasizes the importance of understanding this other definition.

History

The concept of medical tourism is not a new one. The first recorded instance of medical tourism dates back thousands of years to when Greek pilgrims traveled from all over the Mediterranean to the small territory in the Saronic Gulf called Epidauria. This territory was the sanctuary of the healing god Asklepios. Epidauria became the original travel destination for medical tourism. Spa towns and sanitariums may be considered an early form of medical tourism. In eighteenth century England, for example, patients visited spas because they were places with supposedly health-giving mineral waters, treating diseases from gout to liver disorders and bronchitis.

Description

Factors that have led to the increasing popularity of medical travel include the high cost of health care, long wait times for certain procedures, the ease and affordability of international travel, and improvements in both technology and standards of care in many countries.

Medical tourists can come from anywhere in the First World, including Europe, the Middle East, Japan, the United States, and Canada. This is because of their large populations, comparatively high wealth, the high expense of health care or lack of health care options locally, and increasingly high expectations of their populations with respect to health care. An authority at the Harvard Business School recently stated that "medical tourism is promoted much more heavily in the United Kingdom than in the United States".

A forecast by Deloitte Consulting published in August 2008 projected that medical tourism originating in the US could jump by a factor of ten over the next decade. An estimated 750,000 Americans went abroad for health care in 2007, and the report estimated that a million and a half would seek health care outside the US in 2008. The growth in medical tourism has the potential to cost US health care providers billions of dollars in lost revenue.

A large draw to medical travel is convenience and speed. Countries that operate public health-care systems are often so taxed that it can take considerable time to get non-urgent medical care. Using Canada as an example, an estimated 782,936 Canadians spent time on medical waiting lists in 2005, waiting an average of 9.4 weeks. Canada has set waiting-time benchmarks, e.g. 26 weeks for a hip replacement and 16 weeks for cataract surgery, for non-urgent medical procedures.

Additionally, patients are finding that insurance either does not cover orthopedic surgery (such as knee/hip replacement) or imposes unreasonable restrictions on the choice of the facility, surgeon, or prosthetics to be used. Medical tourism for knee/hip replacements has emerged as one of the more widely accepted procedures because of the lower cost and minimal difficulties associated with the travelling to/from the surgery. Colombia provides a knee replacement for about $5,000 USD, including all associated fees, such as FDA-approved prosthetics and hospital stay-over expenses. However, many clinics quote prices that are not all inclusive and include only the surgeon fees associated with the procedure.

According to an article by the University of Delaware publication, Daily:

> *" The cost of surgery in India, Thailand or South Africa can be one-tenth of what it is in the United States or Western Europe, and sometimes even less. A heart-valve replacement that would cost $200,000 or more in the US, for example, goes for $10,000 in India—and that includes round-trip airfare and a brief vacation package. Similarly, a metal-free dental bridge worth $5,500 in the US costs $500 in India, a knee*

replacement in Thailand with six days of physical therapy costs about one-fifth of what it would in the States, and Lasik eye surgery worth $3,700 in the US is available in many other countries for only $730. Cosmetic surgery savings are even greater: A full facelift that would cost $20,000 in the US runs about $1,250 in South Africa."

Popular medical travel worldwide destinations include: Argentina, Brunei, Cuba, Colombia, Costa Rica, Hong Kong, Hungary, India, Jordan, Lithuania, Malaysia, The Philippines, Singapore, South Africa, Thailand, and recently, Saudi Arabia, UAE, South Korea, Tunisia and New Zealand.

Popular cosmetic surgery travel destinations include: Argentina, Bolivia, Brazil, Colombia, Costa Rica, Cuba, Mexico and Turkey. In South America, countries such as Argentina, Bolivia, Brazil and Colombia lead on plastic surgery medical skills relying on their experienced plastic surgeons. In Bolivia and Colombia, plastic surgery has also become quite common. According to the Sociedad Boliviana de Cirugia Plasticay Reconstructiva", more than 70% of middle and upper class women in the country have had some form of plastic surgery. Colombia also provides advanced care in cardiovascular and transplant surgery.

In Europe Belgium, Poland and Slovakia are also breaking into the business. South Africa is taking the term "medical tourism" very literally by promoting their "medical safaris".

A specialized subset of medical tourism is reproductive tourism and reproductive outsourcing, which is the practice of travelling abroad to undergo in-vitro fertilization, surrogate pregnancy and other assisted reproductive technology treatments including freezing embryos for retro-production. However, perceptions of medical tourism are not always positive. In places like the US, which has high standards of quality, medical tourism is viewed as risky. In some parts of the world, wider political issues can influence where medical tourists will choose to seek out health care. Health tourism providers have developed as intermediaries to unite potential medical tourists with provider hospitals and other organisations. Companies are beginning to offer global health care options that will enable North American and European patients to access world health care at a fraction of the cost of domestic care. Companies that focus on medical value travel typically provide nurse case managers to assist patients with pre- and post-travel medical issues. They also help provide resources for follow-up care upon the patient's return.

Process

The typical process is as follows: the person seeking medical treatment abroad contacts a medical tourism provider. The provider usually requires the patient to provide a medical report, including the nature of ailment, local doctor's opinion, medical history, and diagnosis, and may request additional information. Certified medical doctors or consultants then advise on the medical treatment. The approximate expenditure, choice of hospitals and tourist destinations, and duration of stay, etc., is discussed. After signing consent bonds and agreements, the patient is given recommendation letters for a medical visa, to be procured from the concerned embassy. The patient travels to the destination country, where the medical tourism provider assigns a case executive, who takes care of the patient's accommodation, treatment and any other form of care. Once the treatment is done, the patient can remain in the tourist destination or return home.

International Healthcare Accreditation

Because standards are important when it comes to health care, there are parallel issues around medical tourism, international healthcare accreditation, evidence-based medicine and quality assurance.

The oldest international accrediting body is Accreditation Canada, formerly known as the Canadian Council on Health Services Accreditation, which accredited the Bermuda Hospital Board as soon as 1968. Since then, it has accredited hospitals and health service organizations in ten other countries.

In the United States, the best known accreditation group is the Joint Commission International (JCI). They have been inspecting and accrediting health care facilities and hospitals outside of the United States since 1999. Many international hospitals today see obtaining international accreditation as a way to attract American patients.

Joint Commission International is a relative of the Joint Commission in the United States. Both are independent private sector not-for-profit organizations that develop nationally and internationally recognized procedures and standards to help improve patient care and safety. They work with hospitals to help them meet Joint Commission standards for patient care and then accredit those hospitals meeting the standards.

In the UK and Hong Kong, the Trent International Accreditation Scheme is a key player. The different international healthcare accreditation schemes vary in quality, size, cost, intent and the skill and intensity of their marketing. They also vary in terms of cost to hospitals and healthcare institutions making use of them. A forecast by Deloitte Consulting regarding medical tourism published in August 2008 noted the value of accreditation in ensuring quality of healthcare and specifically mentioned JCI, ISQUA and Trent.

Increasingly, some hospitals are looking towards dual international accreditation, perhaps having both JCI to cover potential US clientele, Trent for potential British and European clientele and Accreditation Canada. As a result of competition between clinics for American medical tourists, there have been initiatives to rank hospitals based on patient-reported metrics.

Other organizations providing contributions to quality practices include:

- The Society for International Healthcare Accreditation (SOFIHA), a free-to-join group providing a forum for discussion and for the sharing of ideas and good practice by providers of international healthcare accreditation and users of the same. The primary role of this organisation is to promote a safe hospital environment for patients.
- The United Kingdom Accreditation Forum (UKAF) is an established network of accreditation organisations with

the intention of sharing experience good practice and new ideas around the methodology for accreditation programmes, covering issues such as developing healthcare quality standards, implementation of standards within healthcare organisations, assessment by peer review and exploration of the peer review techniques to include the recruitment, training, monitoring and evaluation of peer reviewers and the mechanisms for awards of accredited status to organisations.

Organizations and Associations

International hospitals, insurance companies and medical travel facilitators have in recent years sought affiliations through various organizations such as the International Medical Travel Association, based in Singapore.

Medical Tourism Association (MTA), the second non-profit trade association for medical tourism (after the International Medical Travel Association), is made up of international hospitals, healthcare providers, medical travel facilitators, insurance companies, and other affiliated companies and members with the common goal of promoting medical tourism in a global environment. The Association promotes the interests of its healthcare provider and medical travel facilitator members. The MTA claims three tenets: Transparency, Communication and Education. These tenets were recently called into question in a Reuters article during the time of one if its conferences. Further questions about the legitimacy of the organization were discussed in an International Medical Travel Journal piece on a legal dispute involving the MTA. Some in the medical tourism industry have complained of unethical or illegal practices such as redirecting non-MTA member web sites to the MTA web site or the MTA claiming to be the sole voice of the entire medical tourism industry.

The goal of these types of associations is often to raise awareness of medical tourism in the hopes of expanding the industry.

Risks

Medical tourism carries some risks that locally-provided medical care does not. Some countries, such as India, Malaysia, or Thailand have very different infectious disease-related epidemiology to Europe and North America.

Exposure to diseases without having built up natural immunity can be a hazard for weakened individuals, specifically with respect to gastrointestinal diseases (e.g. Hepatitis A, amoebic dysentery, paratyphoid) which could weaken progress, mosquito-transmitted diseases, influenza, and tuberculosis. However, because in poor tropical nations diseases run the gamut, doctors seem to be more open to the possibility of considering any infectious disease, including HIV, TB, and typhoid, while there are cases in the West where patients were consistently misdiagnosed for years because such diseases are perceived to be "rare" in the West.

The quality of post-operative care can also vary dramatically, depending on the hospital and country, and may be different from US or European standards. However, JCI and Trent fulfill the role of accreditation by assessing the standards in the healthcare in the countries like India, China and Thailand.

Also, travelling long distances soon after surgery can increase the risk of complications. Long flights and decreased mobility in a cramped airline cabin are a known risk factor for developing blood clots in the legs such as venous thrombosis or pulmonary embolus economy class syndrome. Other vacation activities can be problematic as well — for example, scars may become darker and more noticeable if they sunburn while healing. To minimise these problems, medical tourism patients often combine their medical trips with vacation time set aside for rest and recovery in the destination country.

Also, health facilities treating medical tourists may lack an adequate complaints policy to deal appropriately and fairly with complaints made by dissatisfied patients.

Differences in healthcare provider standards around the world have been recognised by the World Health Organization, and in 2004 it launched the World Alliance for Patient Safety. This body assists hospitals and government around the world in setting patient safety policy and practices that can become particularly relevant when providing medical tourism services.

Legal Issues

Receiving medical care abroad may subject medical tourists to unfamiliar legal issues. The limited nature of litigation in various countries is one reason for the lower cost of care overseas. While some countries currently presenting themselves as attractive medical tourism destinations provide some form of legal remedies for medical malpractice, these legal avenues may be unappealing to the medical tourist. Should problems arise, patients might not be covered by adequate personal insurance or might be unable to seek compensation via malpractice lawsuits. Hospitals and/or doctors in some countries may be unable to pay the financial damages awarded by a court to a patient who has sued them, owing to the hospital and/or the doctor not possessing appropriate insurance cover and/or medical indemnity.

Ethical Issues

There can be major ethical issues around medical tourism. For example, the illegal purchase of organs and tissues for transplantation has been alleged in countries such as India and China prior to 2007. Medical tourism may raise broader ethical issues for the countries in which it is promoted. For example in India, some argue that a "policy of 'medical tourism for the classes and health missions for the masses' will lead to a deepening of the inequities" already embedded in the health care system. In Thailand, in 2008 it was stated that, "Doctors in Thailand have become so busy with foreigners that Thai patients are having trouble getting care". Medical tourism centred on new technologies, such as stem cell treatments, is often criticized on grounds of fraud, blatant lack of scientific rationale and patient safety. However, when pioneering advanced technologies, such as providing 'unproven' therapies to patients outside of regular clinical trials, it is often challenging to differentiate between acceptable medical innovation and unacceptable patient exploitation.

Employer-sponsored Health Care in the US

Some US employers have begun exploring medical travel programs as a way to cut employee health care costs. Such proposals have raised stormy debates between employers and trade unions representing workers, with one union stating that it deplored the "shocking new approach" of offering employees overseas treatment in return for a share of the company's savings. The unions also raise the issues of legal liability should something go wrong, and potential job losses in the US health care industry if treatment is outsourced.

Employers may offer incentives such as paying for air travel and waiving out-of-pocket expenses for care outside of the US. For example, in January 2008, Hannaford Bros., a supermarket chain based in Maine, began paying the entire medical bill for employees to travel to Singapore for hip and knee replacements, including travel for the patient and companion. Medical travel packages can integrate with all types of health insurance, including limited benefit plans, preferred provider organizations and high deductible health plans. In 2000 Blue Shield of California began the United States' first cross border health plan. Patients in California could travel to one of the three certified hospitals in Mexico for treatment under California Blue Shield. In 2007, a subsidiary of BlueCross BlueShield of South Carolina, Companion Global Healthcare, teamed up with hospitals in Thailand, Singapore, Turkey, Ireland, Costa Rica and India. A 2008 article in *Fast Company* discusses the globalization of healthcare and describes how various players in the US healthcare market have begun to explore it.

Subfields

Dental: Dental tourism involves individuals seeking dental care outside of their local healthcare systems.

Fertility: Fertility tourism is the practice of travelling to another country for fertility treatments. The main reasons for fertility tourism are legal regulation of the sought procedure in the home country, or lower price. In-vitro fertilization, donor insemination and surrogacy are major procedures involved.

Destinations

Africa and Middle East

Countries in this region involved in medical tourism include Saudi Arabia, South Africa, and Tunisia.

Israel

Israel is emerging as a popular destination for medical tourists. In 2006, 15,000 foreigners travelled to the country for medical procedures, bringing in $40 million of revenue.

Medical tourists choose Israel for several reasons. Some come from European nations such as Romania where certain procedures are not available. Others come to Israel, perhaps most commonly from the US, because they can receive quality health care at a fraction of the cost it would be at home, for both surgeries and in-vitro fertilization treatments. Other medical tourists come to Israel to visit the Dead Sea, a world-famous therapeutic resort. The Israel Ministry of Tourism and several professional medical services providers have set out to generate awareness of Israel's medical capabilities.

Jordan

Jordan is an emerging medical tourism destination, with related revenues exceeding one billion dollars in 2007. More than 250,000 patients from other countries sought treatment in Jordan that year. This included an estimated 45,000 Iraqis and approximately 25,000 patients each from Palestine and Sudan. An estimated 1,800 US citizens, 1,200 UK citizens, and 400 Canadians also sought treatment in Jordan that year. Treatment costs can be as low as 25 percent of costs in the US. The kingdom was rated as number one in the region and fifth in the world as a medical tourism hub in a study by the World Bank.

UAE

Hospitals in Dubai and other emirates have expressed an intent to develop in medical tourism. Some have American-sourced international healthcare accreditation, while others are looking towards the UK, Australia and Canada for accreditation services.

The Americas

Countries in the Americas that are treating foreign patients include Argentina, Bolivia, Brazil, Colombia, Costa Rica, Cuba, Dominican Republic, Guatemala, Mexico, Panama, Peru and Uruguay.

Brazil

Brazil has long been known as a destination for cosmetic surgery. For non-cosmetic procedures, Brazil is only now entering the global market. However, Albert Einstein Jewish Hospital in Sao Paulo was the first JCI-accredited facility outside of the US, and more than a dozen Brazilian medical facilities have since been similarly accredited. Brazil requires visas for US citizens based on a reciprocal arrangement since Brazilians are required to obtain a visa to visit the US.

Canada

Canada has entered the medical tourism field. In comparison to US health costs, medical tourism patients can save 30 to 60 percent on health costs in Canada.

Cuba

Cuba has been a popular medical tourism destination for more than 40 years. Thousands of patients travel to Cuba, particularly from Latin America and Europe, attracted by the "fine reputation of Cuban doctors, the low prices and nearby beaches on which to recuperate." In 2006, Cuba attracted nearly 20,000 health tourists. Medical treatments included joint replacement, cancer treatment, eye surgery, cosmetic surgery and addictions rehabilitation. Costs are about 60 to 80 percent less than US costs.

Cuba has hospitals for Cuban residents and others that focus on serving foreigners and diplomats. In the 2007 American documentary film, *Sicko*, which criticizes the US healthcare system, producer Michael Moore leads a group of uninsured American patients to Cuba to obtain more affordable medical treatment. *Sicko* has greatly increased foreigners' interest in Cuban healthcare. A recent Miami Herald story focused on the high quality of health care that Canadian and American medical tourism patients receive in Cuba. The Cuban government has developed Cuban medical tourism to generate income for the country. Residents of Canada, the UK and most other countries can travel to Cuba without any difficulty a tourist visa is generally required. For Americans, however, because of the US trade policy towards Cuba, travellers must either obtain US government approval, or, more frequently, travel to Cuba from Canada, Mexico, the Bahamas, Jamaica or the Dominican Republic. Cuban immigration authorities do not stamp the passports of US visitors so that Americans can keep their travels a private matter. To date no Cuban facility has achieved JCI Accreditation.

Mexico

Americans, particularly those living near the Mexican border, now routinely cross to Mexico for medical care. Popular specialties include dentistry and plastic surgery. Mexican dentists often charge one-fifth to one-fourth of US prices, while other procedures typically cost a third what they would in the US.

This trend has alarmed American healthcare providers who, fearing a loss of business, warn patients away from Mexico. "The phenomenon has unsettled US-based dentists who tell horror stories of rampant infections, undetected cases of oral cancer and shoddy work south of the border", claims hotly disputed by Mexican dentists. "In Texas, legislators explored the possibility of allowing health maintenance organizations to operate on both sides of the border. However, physicians in south Texas lobbied against the changes, arguing that local doctors could not compete with the lower costs in Mexico". US doctors point out that the Mexican legal system makes it almost impossible to sue Mexican doctors for malpractice. However, many who travel to Mexico for care report that they are satisfied. According to a report commissioned by Families U.S.A., a Washington advocacy group for health-care issues, "About 90 percent [feel] the care they had received in Mexico had been good or excellent. About 80 percent rated the care they had received in the United States as good or excellent". Indeed "some U.S. dentists ... have conceded to the competition and begun a 'reverse migration' opening offices in Mexico to take advantage of lower costs". More American insurers are providing coverage for travellers, as the out-of-pocket costs to them are much lower. "With healthcare costs in the United States continuing to rise, many employers in Southern California are turning to insurance plans that send their workers to Mexico for routine care, plans that are growing by nearly 3,000 people a year."

In addition to dental and plastic surgery, Mexican hospitals are popular for bariatric surgery for weight loss, considered an elective procedure that is not covered by some US insurers. A popular bariatric procedure, lap band surgery, which was approved by the FDA in the US in 2001, has been performed for longer by Mexican surgeons.

Panama

In Panama, health and medical tourism is growing rapidly. Factors drawing medical tourists include Panama's tourist appeal, position as a hub for international travel, and use of the American dollar as the official currency. Many of Panama's doctors are bilingual, board certified, and accustomed to working with the same medical equipment and technology used in the United States and Europe. On most procedures, Panama offers savings of more than 50% compared to the US and Europe. No Panamanian hospitals currently have international healthcare accreditation, whether through US, British, Australian or Canadian sources.

United States

Although much attention has been given to the growing trend of uninsured Americans travelling to foreign countries, a report from 2008 found that a plurality of an estimated 60,000 to 85,000 medical tourists were travelling to the United States for the purpose of receiving inpatient medical care. The availability of advanced medical technology and sophisticated training of physicians are cited as driving motivators for growth in foreigners travelling to the U.S. for medical care. Also, it has been noted that the decline in value of the U.S. dollar is offering additional incentive for foreign travel to the U.S. However, costs differences between the US and many locations in Asia far outweigh any currency fluctuations.

Several major medical centres and teaching hospitals offer international patient centres that cater to patients from foreign countries who seek medical treatment in the U.S. Many of these organizations offer service coordinators to assist international patients with arrangements for medical care, accommodations, finances and transportation including air ambulance services.

It should be noted that many locations in the US that offer medical care comparable in price to foreign medical facilities are not Joint Commission Accredited.

Uruguay

Uruguay recently entered the medical tourism market. A private medical tourism initiative, Uruhealth, has been created with support from the Ministries of Tourism and Public Health. The initiative involves the infrastructure, human resources and experience of two healthcare companies: MP Personalized Medicine (Montevideo) and SEMM-Mautone Hospital (Punta del Este).

Asia/Pacific

Many Asian Pacific countries are medical tourism destinations.

China

China is fast emerging as a desirable destination for individuals seeking medical care in a wide range of medical specialties, including cardiology, neurology, orthopedics and others. A number of private and government hospitals in major cities have established international departments. Many leading hospitals provide treatments integrating Traditional Chinese Medicine with Western medical technology and techniques. China is home to leading stem cell research and treatment hospitals that offer Westerners who want to take advantage of stem cell treatments that are still considered experimental or have yet to be approved in their home country.

Hong Kong

As of 2006, Hong Kong had 12 private hospitals and 39 public hospitals, providing 3,124 and 27,755 beds respectively. A wide range of health care services are offered. All 12 of Hong Kong's private hospitals have been surveyed and accredited by the UK's Trent Accreditation Scheme since early 2001. This has been a major factor in the ascent of standards in Hong Kong's private hospitals. The Trent scheme works closely with the hospitals it assesses to generate standards appropriate to the locality (with respect to culture, geography, public health, primary care interfaces etc.), and always uses combinations of UK-sourced and Hong Kong-sourced surveyors. Some of Hong Kong's private hospitals have now gone on to obtain dual international accreditation, with both Trent and JCI (and have therefore attained a standard surpassing some of the best hospitals in Thailand and Singapore). Others are looking towards dual international accreditation with Trent and the Australian group. Hong Kong public hospitals have yet to commit to external accreditation.

India

India's medical tourism sector is expected to experience an annual growth rate of 30%, making it a Rs. 9,500-crore industry by 2015. Estimates of the value of medical tourism to India go as high as $2 billion a year by 2012. Advantages for medical tourists include reduced costs, the availability of latest medical technologies and a growing compliance on international quality standards, as well as the fact that foreigners are not likely to face a language barrier in India. The Indian government is taking steps to address infrastructure issues that hinder the country's growth in medical tourism. Most estimates claim treatment costs in India start at around a tenth of the price of comparable treatment in America or Britain. The most popular treatments sought in India by medical tourists are alternative medicine, bone-marrow transplant, cardiac bypass surgery, eye surgery and orthopedic surgery. India is known in particular for heart surgery, hip resurfacing and other areas of advanced medicine. Ministry of Tourism India (MoT) is planning to extend its Market Development Assistance (MDA) scheme to cover Joint Commission International (JCI) and National Accreditation Board of Hospitals (NABH) certified hospitals. A policy announcement of this effect is likely soon. The south Indian city of Chennai is regarded as the healthcare capital of India.

Korea, Republic of

Listed on CNN.com as one of the "hot destinations" for medical tourism, Korea is quickly establishing itself in the field of medical tourism.

However, *The Korea Times* reported in a series of articles that Korean hospitals have adopted a discriminatory pricing policy, charging foreigners two to three times more than the full-fee for locals.

The paper revealed that the price disparity in medical fees for foreign patients is extremely high, considering that the difference between the lowest and highest fees for the most-sought-after procedures exceeds more than 10 times on average.

It claims the government is overlooking soaring medical fees on foreign patients, who are unprotected from malpractice, discriminatory charging, overpricing and patient privacy rights under the Korean Medical Law.

In 2008, Korea had 27,480 foreign-based patients and the Korean health ministry expects that number to increase to 140,000 by 2015. Due to legislation passed in May 2009, state-licensed clinics and hospitals are now allowed to directly seek out foreign patients through various promotional activities.

Korean hospitals and clinics provide a variety of medical services for medical tourists including comprehensive health screening, cancer treatment, organ transplantation, joint/ rheumatism care, spinal treatment, ophthalmology, dental care, infertility treatment, otorhinolaryngology, and Korean traditional medicine. Currently, the most popular treatments for medical tourists are cosmetic procedures such as eyelid surgery, nose jobs, facelifts, and skin lightening.

Over 30 Korean hospitals and clinics are member providers under the Council for Korea Medicine Overseas Promotion (CKMOP). Among these facilities are the "Big Four" – Seoul National University Hospital, Samsung Medical Centre, Asan Medical Centre, and Yonsei Severance Hospital.

Malaysia

Malaysia is well on its way to develop itself as a medical tourism hub. The country has excellent hospitals, English is widely spoken, and many staff have been trained to a high level in the UK or in the US. There is a highly active Association for Private Hospitals of Malaysia working to develop medical tourism. However, while Malaysia has a national accreditation healthcare scheme (MSQH) and many Malaysia's hospitals are currently firmly on the way to achieve international healthcare accreditation.

Malaysian hospitals International Specialist Eye Centre, Penang Adventist Hospital and many others such as Gleneagles Hospital Kuala Lumpur have or are going to be JCI accredited. The Ministry of Health has launched a medical tourism page with medical tourism portals such as Wellness Visit.

New Zealand

New Zealand is a relatively new destination to medical travel. It has all the hallmarks of a very successful destination especially for North American based patients. This includes being a first world, developed economy with a sophisticated and comprehensive medical system. It is first and foremost English speaking with a rich heritage of producing world class doctors and medical research.

Many of its private hospitals are internationally accredited, state of the art and offer an integrated package of care. The surgeons in New Zealand are trained both in New Zealand and abroad, usually spending years of their training in either North America or Western Europe.

While New Zealand is aligned medically and culturally to North America, the cost of the surgical care is significantly cheaper. On average it is considered that New Zealand's surgical costs are around 15 to 20% the cost of the same surgical procedure in the USA. One patient who had his prosthetic hip replaced in New Zealand said the total cost including travel, lodging and the surgery at a private hospital was $20,000, as opposed to the $80,000 - $140,000 he was told the operation would have cost at home.

Added to this the personalized level of medical care, the world renown natural beauty and tranquility, the fact that New Zealand is one of the safest places in the world and only 12 hours direct flight from the west coast of North America, then New Zealand as a medical travel destination looks set to develop.

Philippines

The Philippines has been growing as a destination for medical tourism. The US Medical Tourism Association magazine reported that this services sub-sector grew 8.0% in 2007. The number can be expected to grow as American health-care costs rise, or if pending legislation results in an increase in patient wait times for surgical procedures (as has been seen in other countries where care has been nationalized), due to the traditional political, economic and cultural connections between the United States and the Philippines. The Philippines is one of a few countries that sends qualified nurses, physicians and dentists to the US, the thousands serving in American medical facilities being a testament to its quality of medical education. According to year 2000 WHO rankings of the world's health systems, the Philippines takes its position on no.60.

Singapore

Singapore has a dozen hospitals and health centres with JCI accreditation. In 1997 (published 2000), the World Health Organization ranked Singapore's health care system sixth best in the world and the highest ranked system in Asia. "Singapore Medicine" is a multi-agency government-industry partnership committed to strengthening Singapore's position as a medical hub and promoting Singapore as a destination for advanced patient care. Patients come from neighboring countries, such as Indonesia and Malaysia, and patient numbers from Indochina, South Asia, the Middle East and Greater China are growing. Patients from developed countries such as the United States and the UK are also beginning to choose Singapore as their medical travel destination for relatively affordable health care services in a clean cosmopolitan city.

Taiwan

The Taiwanese government has declared its determination for the country to become a medical tourism centre. In 2007, the Department of Health launched a campaign to promote inbound medical tourism, focusing on integrating the resources of the government and academia to build Taiwan's brand as a medical tourism destination. Costs for procedures remain comparatively low. Taiwan is known for liver transplants, joint replacement surgery, bone marrow transplants, and reconstructive and plastic surgery.

Thailand

Medical tourism has been a growing segment of Thailand's tourism and health-care sectors. In 2005, one Bangkok hospital took in 150,000 treatment seekers from abroad. In 2006, medical tourism was projected to earn the country 36.4 billion baht.

Treatments for medical tourists in Thailand range from cosmetic, organ transplants, cardiac, and orthopaedic treatments to dental and cardiac surgeries. Treatments also include spa, physical and mental therapies. One patient who had coronary artery bypass surgery at Bumrungrad International hospital in Bangkok said the operation cost him US$12,000 (8,200 euros), as opposed to the $100,000 (68,000 euros) he estimated the operation would have cost him at home.

Bumrungrad treated approximately 55,000 American patients in 2005 alone, a 30% increase from the previous year. Hospitals in Thailand are a popular destination for other Asians. Bangkok Hospital, which caters to medical tourists, has a Japanese wing, and Phyathai Hospitals Group has interpreters for over 22 languages, besides the English-speaking medical staff. When Nepal Prime Minister Girija Prasad Koirala needed medical care in 2006, he went to Bangkok.

Many Thai physicians hold US or UK professional certification. Bumrungrad International hospital states that many of its doctors and staff are trained in the UK, Europe and the US. Bumrungrad International was accredited most recently in 2005 by the Joint Commission. Some of the country's major hospitals have also achieved certification by the International Organization for Standardization's ISO 9001:2000. However, ISO 2000 is not an accreditation scheme.

The World Health Organization's 2000 ranking put the Thai healthcare system at number 47, below the USA's ranking at 37 and the United Kingdom's ranking at 18.

Serious political problems during late 2008, including mass

demonstrations and the complete closure of major airports, have made travel to Thailand less appealing than in the past, and the US State Department has issued a travel alert for the country.

Europe

Countries in Europe that have active medical tourism sectors include Turkey, Cyprus, Germany, Hungary, Lithuania, Malta, Poland, Portugal, Czech Republic, Slovakia, Spain, and Ukraine.

Czech Republic

Czech Republic has built its medical tourism on spas and medical care equalling the world standards.

Germany

Germany is a destination for patients seeking advanced medical technology, high standards, safety, and quick treatment. All German citizens have health coverage, resulting in a high hospital density, with twice as many hospitals per capita as the United States. The high hospital density results in shorter waitlists for treatment. Costs for medical treatment compete well with other developed European countries and are commonly 50% of those in in the USA.

Germany is an attractive destination for patients from the Middle East since travelling to the USA has become more difficult for them since the September 11 attacks. US citizens sometimes travel to Germany to seek treatments such as artificial cervical disc replacement that are not US Food and Drug Administration (FDA) approved.

Poland

Since 2004, when Poland joined the European Union, it has become another locale for people seeking cheaper medical treatments. The quality of care in Poland must comply with EU standards.

Turkey

Turkey has since many years attracted medical tourists from Europe and the Balkans, the United States, Eurasia and the Middle East.

The Turkish private healthcare system is striving to become a strategic global health service provider manufacturing centre. The site contains information on prices and hospital statistics, information about the healthcare, pharmaceutical and insurance environments as well as an international patient guide.

Turkey has the highest number of JCI accredited healthcare institutions in the world except for the US. The German Hospital in Istanbul operates the country's first ISO-certified IVF centre, while Memorial Hospital was the first private hospital to receive American JCI accreditation. Since then, over 34 hospitals and medical institutions have achieved Joint Commission International accreditation.

2

E-Business in the Hospitality

Introduction

As hospitality industry executives contemplate the launch of the new millennium, they need to recognize the huge changes that are occurring in the way business is being conducted and begin planning in earnest as to how they will respond.

For those operating within the physical world, the concept of electronic business or "e-business" may appear to be of limited significance. But such an assumption could be costly. E-business and its applications are undoubtedly the No. 1 topic in the boardrooms of most of the world's largest companies. The financial markets are making massive investments in the companies that deliver Internet technologies, content and related products and services, and the corporate world is now moving toward e-business offerings at a rapid clip.

On the business-to-business (b-to-b) front, e-business is projected to grow enormously in the United States over the next several years, with business-to-consumer (b-to-c) trade not as big, but growing just as fast. The McKenna Group estimates that the b-to-b marketplace could grow in value to US$500 billion in 2003. But those estimates may be low. General Motors Corporation, Ford Motor Company and Daimler Chrysler, for example, have just announced that they plan to combine their efforts to form a b-to-b integrated supplier exchange through a single global portal. Meanwhile, on the retail front, the race is on to win the Internet consumer, whose ranks are growing rapidly.

Traditional retailers have much to be concerned about as retail sales over the Internet skyrocket. And while such activity has yet to grow to the same extent in Europe and Asia/Pacific where the cost of phone calls remains an issue, it surely will over time. In the meantime, travel is one of the more popular online products for sale and over the next several years, it is projected in the United States alone to grow to US$12 billion.

E-business is rewriting the economic rules globally for every industry-including hospitality, travel and leisure. Indeed, it's important to recognize that we are now operating in what has been described as the "new economy," as global trends drive change, including globalization, consolidation, convergence, technology and communications. Even more, it is clear that the underlying sources of value are also changing. Use of intangible assets such as information, brands, customers, relationships and networks distinguish the most successful companies in the world.

The Impact of the Internet

It is clear that the Internet is having a huge impact on how we conduct our lives and our businesses. And it arrived virtually overnight. In the United States, for example, it took 38 years for television to get into 50 million homes. For the Internet, it took just five years. And for those U.S. consumers that are online, four out of five believe that the Internet is a more important invention than television. Of these same online consumers, close to six in 10 prefer e-mail to paper mail for business correspondence and over one in four check their e-mail while on vacation.

The Internet is also changing the customer relationship-undermining and redirecting customer attention to new sellers of products and services and away from their traditional relationships. And as this occurs, the traditional approaches that hospitality businesses have taken to distribution are all being affected. From reservations taken over the Internet, which are projected to more than double to 9% of volume over the next year, to the declining role of the travel agent.

This occurs as so-called "infomediaries" provide information and access, and software robots troll the activity online to develop matches between buyers and sellers, analyzing complex patterns and looking for trends for marketers to capitalize upon. As for the infomediaries, we can expect some of these to move into the transactions business and continue the process of disintermediation. For some hospitality companies, it may be best to join this new competition, particularly if it cannot be beaten at its own game.

The reality today is that the balance of power is shifting from sellers to buyers and in so doing it makes the importance of delivering high-quality service, convenience and value for money ever more compelling.

The Internet has clearly levelled the playing field by making price information broadly available to the consumer. Internet business models affect product and services offerings, pricing, distribution and customer service, as well as long-term information capabilities. As a consequence, some hospitality suppliers will inevitably feed different tranches of their inventory through the various channels at their disposal-including the Internet, travel management organizations, destination packagers and the like.

Convenience and Consistency

In the end, customers want both convenience and consistency. They don't have all the leisure time that futurists once predicted they would have by now. In fact, they have less. Today's fast-paced world produces ever more stress, and consumers want information and they want it fast. And if hospitality companies and travel providers don't deliver convenience, somebody else inevitably will. They also want to be wired up to the rest of the world-at home, in their office and especially when they travel. And for hoteliers trying to cope with in-room technologies and the delivery of high-speed Internet access, we will soon be seeing more integration of network communication and entertainment products to further complicate or liberate our lives, depending on your point of view.

Customers are also looking for consistency-a simple concept, but central to whether a brand has value or not. And in the emerging networked world, aligning the value propositions of alliance partners and ensuring a seamless and consistent experience will only be as good as the weakest link in the chain.

New Business Rules are Emerging

Within this new economy, the operating environment for hospitality companies is changing. There are new rules of conduct, new relationships and new criteria for success, along with a new set of metrics. The revolution that we must now confront is therefore no less significant than the one that our forebears had to deal with as the Industrial Revolution changed how people lived, worked and dealt with each other. And like our distant relatives of centuries ago, there are boundless opportunities and countless risks, most obscured within an environment of great uncertainty. In such an era there are certain traits to business behavior that will distinguish success from failure. At this stage in the new economy's evolution, these traits would appear to include speed, agility and flexibility.

Speed is necessary to get to market early with a first-mover advantage that assures early adoption by an increasingly fickle, restless and frequently disloyal customer. Such speed is imperative as so-called "start-up" companies come to dominate their chosen niche in extremely short periods of time, frequently preempting the opportunity for those too slow to react.

Agility is required to be able to respond to competitive threats by not only those we know and can monitor, but also unseen competitors. These latter competitors may not even exist as yet, but as they emerge, they may quickly disintermediate established customer relationships.

And, finally, flexibility is needed to reorganize the established models of business and all of the related processes, and adapt the organization in organic fashion to a new environment in whatever form it takes.

From Place to Space

For business executives at large, one of the most compelling changes that has confronted them in recent years is the potential for e-business. But while the significance of these new media are all too apparent, the business solutions required to capitalize on opportunities they offer are unfortunately not. For most hospitality executives, the essential frame of reference has been a geocentric one where real estate and geography have been the big drivers in a physical world-buildings, dots on maps, markets served, chains. In tomorrow's world, these concepts will require some fundamental adjustments to provide for market "spaces" rather than "places" as the nature of relationships between hotel businesses, their customers, their suppliers and their alliance partners go through rapid and constant change.

As these changes occur, the new economy's business leaders must quickly learn the new rules of the game and adjust their approaches accordingly. And the most successful among us will align key processes around the Internet, build corporate intelligence automatically, create integrated value chains and develop new processes to deal with an ever-changing set of circumstances.

The Human Capital Challenge

Supporting the changes in the new economy will be a vast pool of talented human capital anxious to bring new ideas and new technologies to bear on the traditional ways of doing business and, in doing so, steadily increase the pace of productivity improvement. And if the hospitality industry is to respond to this coming reality, it will need to address some of its most vexing challenges-particularly those relating to the recruitment, training and development of human capital.

The human capital inventory for an e-business will require entrepreneurship, as well as visionary leadership, strength in sales and marketing and commitment to customer relationship management. The organizational bias will need to be toward creativity and risk-taking, and away from dependency on analysis and procedures.

In addition to the human capital challenge, many of today's legacy organizations are better structured to work in the old economy, but are considerably less aligned for many activities in the "new." The cultural challenges may in fact be no less daunting than those presented by some of the technological ones. For large organizations attempting a major shift in orientation, the presence of a significant culture may turn out to be quite a hindrance.

Redefining the Hospitality Business

In some industries, profits are made on spare parts and maintenance rather than on mainstream products. In the new economy, we may see this business model replicated in the hospitality industry. And for those companies that discount or give away products such as hotel rooms in order to sell linked services, they surely will be redefining the meaning of hospitality. They will also be marketing an array of hospitality and leisure products and services to a customer base that is no longer satisfied with the traditional ways of making such purchases.

Hospitality businesses that traditionally provided room, board, management and marketing may need to rethink their roles in the new economy, particularly as services become more valuable than products. With the rapid growth of "infomediaries" and their facilitation of transactions, hospitality businesses may need to redefine themselves in order to prosper in an increasingly electronic world where one-to-one customization is the order of the day. But for those contemplating repositioning their companies in an e-business environment, it will be necessary to focus on the current value proposition of the business and determine how it might be reformatted or enhanced to ensure success in the new setting.

Is the Industry Prepared?

But just how prepared is the global hospitality industry to capitalize on some of the opportunities afforded by the emerging new economy? In Arthur Andersen's recently published global survey of technology, Hospitality 2000: The Technology, we addressed some of the issues that the industry is facing. These included the closed nature of our technology architectures, the way in which we collect information on our customers, our investments in Internet, intranet and extranet technologies, and our adoption of electronic commerce. The results are not especially encouraging and suggest an industry still relatively slow to adapt to e-business. Only 39% of the industry's Web sites, for example, can handle reservations on a real-time basis, and even fewer still (19%), collect customer information. At the same time, just 22% are using "push" marketing programs and a distinct minority (just 19%), have extranets to suppliers or customers. But these adoption rates are nonetheless projected to grow and we should, therefore, expect our industry's leaders to be far more attuned to the needs of an e-business environment in the years to come.

As information technology (IT) is used to facilitate a company's entry into the world of electronic commerce, our industry's leadership will also need to overcome a natural tendency to be disappointed by the role of IT in achieving competitive advantage. For many years IT was seen as a mechanism to support back office finance and accounting functions.

In the future, it inevitably will be one of the principal drivers of value creation in the new economy. But we should not be mislead by IT-in e-business, it will be the strategy, not the technology that will make the difference between success and failure. But having the strategy in place is only the first step. It must be linked to every part of the business.

Planning for e-Business

With the costs of playing in the e-business world escalating rapidly, hospitality executives should consider the four phases of what might be called the "E-Business Lifecycle." The first of these-E-Business Strategy Development and Planning-must address the market and competitive context, articulate the vision and opportunity, outline the strategy and the business case, and identify the risks. In recent years, we have frequently seen hospitality businesses put up a Web site on the Internet and consider this an e-business strategy. But without a strategy for this new form of commerce and the business planning process to drive it, such reactionary approaches stand little chance for success.

Once the plan is in place, an e-business design phase can commence to address site design, lay out the business architecture, identify the technical infrastructure, plan for performance, availability and capacity, and deal with tax issues and enterprise security.

Following the design phase, E-Business implementation will prepare for the launch with training and change enablement, implementation and integration, testing and roll-out. Once in place, E-Business Operations will need to be supported by IT and audit services, Web site activity analysis and Web site maintenance. Finally, measurement systems will need to be established to monitor performance.

As industry executives embark on this e-business lifecycle, they will need in the first stage to clearly establish the business case for investing in new technologies, systems and organizations by addressing both the cost reduction and revenue enhancement benefits. On the revenue side, there are a number of factors to consider. These include the company's ability to identify and recruit the most valuable customers; the ability to seamlessly cross-sell the company's products and services, as well as those of alliance partners; the ability to retain valuable customers and reduce attrition (especially relevant in a world of questionable brand loyalty); and finally, when and how to eliminate costly and unnecessary discounts through revenue optimization.

In this kind of environment, the property management system will no longer hold sway as the centre of the hospitality universe, but will become just one in a series of customer touch-points that will increasingly include the Internet. These touch-points will ultimately need to be fully integrated into a customer information system supported by sophisticated data warehousing and data mining technologies.

Adding to the industry's costs in this portrait of the future is the cost of grafting e-business technologies onto the industry's legacy systems. At a certain stage, it may make sense to start from scratch and ensure that every system is Web-enabled. This would allow a total interface for a high-growth e-business, thereby maximizing the customer relationship management opportunities that it presents.

Success on the Internet

As to the role of the Internet, its comprehensive reach and ubiquitous nature has already ensured its central place in the new economy. But how should we evaluate whether an Internet application is deserving of our attention? Firstly, productivity on the Internet in the years to come will be vastly improved by much higher bandwidth than is currently in place. And with higher bandwidth will come applications that can benefit from such extra capacity delivering tightly focused and reliable content to an increasingly sophisticated and demanding e-customer. If an Internet application is to succeed in the future, it will therefore need to be designed to capitalize on this coming reality.

Secondly, an Internet application needs to form a community of some sort because without a sense of place, albeit of the virtual sort participants will not have that all-important sense of belonging. And as with the industrial revolution, which drew a disparate population to centers of economic activity, so will such "intranet communities" grow in value as their populations increase in size and their economic product expands. For larger businesses that form such communities, they are developing new revenue sources and are reinventing their relationships with customers, employees, suppliers and partners. Smaller companies intent on participating in this new environment, may need to be content as a participant in an established community, rather than trying to take on the creation of a community itself. It is better, perhaps, to be one of many players in a successful space than struggling to establish an identity in a world surrounded by also-rans.

Whether large or small, community developers and marketers of the virtual sort will have to recognize that what may have appeared cool in the physical world to generations brought up in the old economy will not work in the world of e-business. Being cool and staying that way in order to get and keep attention will remain a constant challenge, especially for those keen to nurture a younger generation of travellers brought up on MTV and the Web.

Finally, the successful Internet application needs to improve service while reducing transaction costs, particularly as the balance of power in the buy/sell relationship continues its inexorable migration from sellers to buyers. Service improvement strategies will be nothing new for hospitality businesses, but it is noteworthy that service (rather than on-time delivery, price or other concerns) is the top factor that encourages return e-business.

This must be an area of focus since the current growth of e-business appears destined to outpace the supporting infrastructure and its related service at least over the short term. But as hospitality executives know, delivering good service can be expensive. Scaling the types of service response to the circumstances is a growing need, but one that can be modulated if the value of each customer can be distinguished and the response adjusted accordingly.

In considering the opportunities in hospitality e-business, industry leaders should take stock of the dynamics that are occurring in the new economy and plan accordingly. It is probably easy to dismiss the e-business world as a playground for others with products and services that are more obviously applicable. But our industry is changing, as is the world around us. And as alliance partners, vendors, customers, employees and systems all become Web-enabled, hospitality companies must adjust their strategies, organizations, processes and technologies accordingly.

Bottom Line Rules with Extended Stay

The demand for extended-stay lodging has existed since travellers with a little money in their pocket have had both the time and the inclination to spend time away from homes and businesses. The extended-stay concept dates back to 19th century England when visitors arrived at rooming houses in horse-drawn carriages, and travel was a more leisurely affair than it is today.

Today, the extended-stay lodging sector offers diverse products that vary widely throughout the world to serve the needs of modern leisure and business travellers. And while product offerings differ on the two sides of the Atlantic, there is some consensus on the definition of extended stay. This hotel sector in a variety of forms is made up of commercially run lodging properties with suites or apartments comprising one or more rooms.

As the hospitality industry enters the 21st century, extended stay represents a significant opportunity for hotel companies, developers and investors. Interest in extended stay has been spurred by high net income margins and occupancy rates that typically surpass hotel industry averages. Indeed, extended-stay lodging can be seen as a "win-win" situation for the hotel owner and investors. Higher occupancy rates, lower construction costs and shorter periods of stabilization paint an attractive picture for hoteliers in Europe and the United States. In London, for example, occupancy levels for extended-stay properties are actually better than the already strong levels posted by conventional hotels. In the United States, extended stay was reinvented as a commercial enterprise when Marriott opened its first Residence Inn in 1974. Now, the economics of the extended-stay sector have made it a magnet for real estate investment trusts (REITs) and other investment groups in hospitality.

This article draws a profile of the extended-stay lodging sector as it has evolved in the United States and Europe, with the focus on its current state of development and economic opportunity in the future.

What is Extended Stay?

Extended-stay properties operate under several banners, but generally fall into one of three categories:

- all-suite hotels;
- apartment hotels or aparthotels; and
- serviced apartments.

The traditions and definitions of extended-stay lodging, however, differ from country to country. All-suite hotels, featuring the full range of services available at a first-class hotel in the United States, are typically not considered a part of extended-stay lodging in Europe. The apartment hotel (or aparthotel) is primarily a European term. They are popular with tourists in resort areas. Serviced apartments, which are known as corporate housing in the United States, are described as boarding houses in Germany. In Eastern European cities, the term also identifies single apartments found in various buildings that are marketed and serviced by an operator. The lexicon of extended stay in its many variations can be attributed in part to its history of development. In the United

States, extended-stay lodging has been adopted by the hotel industry as an extension of hotel lodging. Hotel companies such as Marriott have begun to penetrate the corporate housing sector with extended-stay properties for business use.

As extended stay was reinvented as an extension of the hotel industry, it has continued to be identified as a complementary commercial enterprise annexed to U.S. hotel development. In contrast, the sector in Europe has grown as a separate business concept, particularly in Great Britain and France. And in Germany, the segment emerged as a product diversification among real estate developers in the early 1990s when hotels and housing were not too attractive to investors, but the combination of the two seemed to hold a potential for good returns.

Varying definitions of extended-stay lodging in Europe and the United States are also reflected in the type and volume of performance data available. In the United States, data has been developed on this segment of the hospitality industry. In Europe, however, the prevalence of serviced apartments with widely varying sites, locations and contract terms, as well as the limited supply of apartment hotels and the small markets in some cities, make it hard to obtain performance statistics and even harder to compare cities or countries from market to market.

Location

The development patterns of extended stay are also distinctly different in U.S. and European markets. European serviced apartments have traditionally been located in city centers with strong, all-season tourist and business demand. Catering mostly to leisure travellers, apartment hotels were initially unbranded. The easy availability of transportation was of primary concern. Establishing extended-stay lodging in major cities meant that many properties were converted, rather than purpose-built, offering fewer and smaller units than comparable properties in the United States. The major European aparthotel brands, Orion and Citadines, began to expand domestically in France in the late 1980s, and internationally in the early 1990s when they opened properties in Belgium, Spain, Portugal and the United Kingdom. In many cases, the bulk of supply is in the capital cities. In the United States, however, preferred extended-stay product locations are often suburban areas, usually close to suburban office parks, hospitals or senior residence communities. Southern locations fare better, mainly due to the high volume of relocation, both by companies and their employees, and by senior citizens. Although used by leisure guests, most extended-stay accommodation is located so as to be convenient to business travellers. Moreover, it has taken U.S. operators much longer to build up the domestic market and move to international locations than their European counterparts.

The difference in location types between the United States and Europe relates to the varying patterns of settlement and the level of dependence on cars. The general preference for urban locations in Europe has important implications for the economics of the projects, since land prices will typically be much higher in central areas and available plots tend to be smaller. In general, the downtown locations have meant conversions and nontraditional solutions to space and configuration problems, rather than new construction.

The greatly varying development patterns and economics in the United States and Europe will, undoubtedly, continue to translate into varying risks and rewards for developers of extended stay properties.

U.S. most Highly Developed

The U.S. extended-stay market, the world's most developed, is primarily comprised of three extended-stay products: (1) all-suite hotels; (2) limited-service hotels, and (3) serviced apartments, the corporate housing market.

The all-suite hotel is relatively common in metropolitan areas and refers to full-service hotels with two-room units, usually with a bedroom and living room. These hotels have limited public areas and services. The apartment hotel, as its name implies, is equipped with a kitchen or kitchenette and may have one or two rooms. These hotels are often in the budget or economy class. They are typically described under the limited-service concept because they usually have fewer staff on site with food and beverage limited to a breakfast room, and they do not report food and beverage revenue. Serviced apartments-intended for the corporate housing market-are generally considered separate from the extended-stay lodging sector. Properties in this category vary widely in size, even in the same location. They have fully equipped kitchens and service is limited to daytime reception and weekly or biweekly cleaning. Typically there are no public areas such as lounges and breakfast rooms.

Supply. In the United States, there is a clear segmentation of extended-stay products among upper-, mid-and lower-tier properties, based on servicing and pricing. The pioneers in extended stay developed first-class properties. But with the increased mobility of middle-class travellers, the volume of business travel and the entry of franchise companies into the market, new brands and operators have emerged in the lower price/service tiers. The largest U.S. extended-stay hotel operators, such as Marriott and Extended-Stay America (ESA), commonly have multiple brands in each segment. In 1998, the extended-stay supply in the United States comprised 137,500 units. Of those units:

- Thirty-nine percent were in the upper tier; Marriott Residence Inn dominated that market with 303 properties.
- Twenty-nine percent fell into the mid-tier with ESA's Studio Plus at the top with 86 properties.
- Thirty-seven fell into the lower tier, with ESA leading with 222 properties.

A short history of extended-stay in the United States offers insights into the market's expansion with mid-and lower-tier properties leading in that growth. According to Smith Travel Research, upscale room supply increased by 75% between 1994 and 1998, compared to 600% for lower-category stock. The growth trend continued in 1999: by mid-year there were 179,300 rooms in extended stay properties, a 25% increase over mid-1998. Of the 30,300 rooms in the pipeline in late 1999, 37% were in the budget and economy segment, and 31% in the mid-price segment. Analysts estimate total extended-stay supply to increase to 300,000-320,000 rooms by the end of 2002, or 8% of projected hotel room supply.

Growth has been especially rapid during the last two or three years in areas with high population growth, technology industries and rapid rates of immigration. As a result, extended-stay lodging comprises up to 13% of total rooms supply in some southern cities and 9% in metropolitan centers, in contrast to only 3% of total lodging supply on a national basis.

The economics of success. Analysts expect the supply of extended-stay products to continue to grow by some 40,000 to 50,000 units per year until 2003. The interest in the sector is spurred by high net income margins and occupancy rates that typically surpass hotel industry averages. In 1998, extended-stay upper-and lower-tier properties achieved 78% and 67% occupancy, respectively. This stands in sharp contrast to the industry as a whole, which averaged 64% occupancy.

Major players that once dominated the extended-stay market are being joined by REITs and franchise companies, which have been lured by the attraction of the bottom line. Higher occupancy rates, lower construction costs and shorter periods of stabilization have caught the eye of these new entrants.

Construction costs are lower because no money is spent on common area design and construction, plus the initial land costs are lower. The stabilization period tends to be shorter than hotels of comparable quality because of lower operational costs, reduced payroll, and the elimination of low-profit centers such as restaurants. Net operating income (NOI) margins of 50% are not uncommon.

More Players: the Corporate Housing Market

High mobility in the U.S. business sector has created a strong corporate housing market. Oakwood Corporate Housing, founded in 1969, is the world's largest serviced apartment agent and operator with more than 20,000 units in the United States, Thailand, the Philippines, China, and Britain. Large U.S. agents include CRS Corporate Housing, Preferred Living, Apartment Connection, and Corporate Housing Connection. On the Internet, two major search directories for U.S cities are now provided by Rent Net and Showcase Suites.

Some U.S.-based agents market properties worldwide. The largest are BridgeStreet Accommodations (4,000 units in the United States, Canada, Britain, France), Barclay International Group (Europe, the United States, Mexico, Israel) and Global Home Network (London, Paris, Prague).

The Extended-Stay Concept Dates back to 19th Century England

The extended-stay concept dates back to 19th century England and a more leisurely approach to travel than today. Now, this diverse sector primarily caters to the corporate executive needing a suite or apartment with one or more rooms.

Great Britain's Market Thriving

In the United Kingdom, serviced apartments are the most common extended-stay product, but aparthotels are increasing in number. Initially the units were designed for the corporate executive or the affluent traveller, but a growing number of mid-level properties have become available during the past few years.

Supply. London represents the most highly developed corporate market in the United Kingdom, as well as Europe at large. Extended-stay supply includes 54% high-end accommodation, while 46% are mid-level properties, which are overwhelmingly located in the West End areas of Mayfair, Kensington and Knightsbridge. The aparthotel market is primarily identified by two brands: Orion and Citadines, both part of Westmont Hospitality. The largest serviced-apartment players are Park Lane Apartments with nine properties and the Cheval Group with four properties. As chain operators enter the market, consolidation and attention to branding may be expected.

Market segmentation in the United Kingdom is not based on price, as is often the case in the United States, but rather more on the size and services required by the predominant group of guests. For instance, there are properties that cater specifically to guests from the Middle East who spend the summer in London with their families and prefer finely appointed apartments with multiple bedrooms.

Extended Stay in London

London	*Units*	*Properties*
Apartment Hotels	300	4
Serviced Apartments		
High-end	1,600	44
Mid-level	1,100	12
Total	3,000	60

Source: Arthur andersen estimates.

The economics of success. Extended-stay occupancy levels in the United Kingdom are typically between 80% and 90%. As in the United States, those levels are somewhat higher than the already strong occupancy levels of hotels in London. Serviced apartments have prospered because of stable tourist and business demand for the product. The high quality of furnishings and spaciousness of the apartments have resulted in high rental rates. Hotels have also recognized the increasing market interest in serviced apartments and several have converted rooms into apartments for extended-stay use. Additionally, operational and marketing synergies make the construction of serviced apartments adjacent to a hotel good strategy.

Marketing. U.K.-based agents, such as Foxtons typically have international operations. The locations covered vary in scope from just a few properties in European capitals (Holiday Serviced Apartments) to offerings around the globe through partner affiliations (The Apartment Service). Some agents, however, are still concentrating on the domestic market and have only limited international offers (Regency Apartments).

Canada's Hospitality Sector: Consolidation

Canada marks the millennium with celebrations spanning the country, from the Atlantic coast to the Pacific islands of British Columbia. In fact, the Millennium Foundation of Canada was the world's first organization dedicated to creating legacies to mark the year 2000. Moreover, Canada's hospitality sector is enjoying a strong run up to the millennium, with solid occupancy rates and a robust domestic economy-a 3.3% annual growth rate-fuelling business travel. With the Canadian dollar hovering about US$0.67 for most of the past two years, Americans and other international travellers have discovered that Canada is a great bargain. Domestic travellers, whose spending power abroad has been significantly diminished, agree.

The result has been healthy occupancy rates in the lodging industry in many major markets across the country. In Toronto, for instance, average annual occupancy has reached a 75%, and tourist and convention spending was more than C$6.4 billion during the past year.

These positive fundamentals have not been lost on the major industry players, who through the driving force of consolidation are beginning to dominate Canada's hospitality market. During the last year, Canadian Pacific, Westmont Corp., Intrawest and others have made significant moves in their attempts to lead their industry sectors:

Canadian Pacific: In May 1998, Canadian Pacific acquired Delta Hotels, which managed or franchised approximately 10,000 rooms at 34 properties. In the deal, Canadian Pacific Hotels acquired the management company and the Delta brand, as well as leasehold interests in three properties for C$93 million. This was followed in late 1998 with the acquisition of the seven warm weather resorts of Princess Hotels from Lonrho Plc for US$540 million.

Canadian Pacific then entered into an agreement with Fairmont Hotel Management LP, creating a new hotel management company called Fairmont Hotels and Resorts Inc.

This new company will manage 69 hotels, including trophy assets such as The Plaza Hotel in New York, The Fairmont in San Francisco, and The Fairmont Copley Plaza in Boston.

Canadian Pacific also continues to add prestigious domestic properties to its portfolio. These include a purchase and renovation of Le Manoir Richelieu in June 1999, which recently re-opened, as well as a new Fairmont Vancouver Airport Place, which opened in October 1999.

Based in Toronto, Canadian Pacific is Canada's largest owner-operator of full service hotels, with approximately 26,000 rooms at 69 properties and 21,500 employees across Canada, the U.S., Mexico, Bermuda, Barbados and Asia.

Westmont Corp.: Industry consolidation continued into the spring of 1999, when UniHost Corp. was acquired by Westmont Corp. At the time, UniHost had the second largest multi-brand hotel operation in Canada and was among the top 10 globally, with a portfolio of 12,000 rooms at 122 properties–102 owned and the balance managed. This would be added to Westmont's existing portfolio of 8,500 rooms at 45 properties across Canada. The group now manages a wide variety of brands, including Comfort, Crowne Plaza, Holiday Inn, Holiday Inn Select, Marriott and Quality.

Westmont Corp. is operated in partnership between the Westmont Hospitality Group, which owns and operates more than 300 hotels in Canada, the U.S. and Europe, and Whitehall Street Real Estate Funds, which is managed by Goldman, Sachs & Co., New York.

Intrawest Corp.: In mid-1999, Vancouver-based Intrawest Corp., the owner of 10 mountain resorts, including Mammoth and Squaw Valley in the U.S. and the Whistler/Blackcomb all-season resort in British Columbia, purchased 50% of Blue Mountain Resorts Ltd., the largest mountain resort in Ontario. In other skiing niche-related news, ClubCorp Resorts, the world's largest owner and operator of private clubs and golf resorts, sold Mont-Sainte-Anne, a ski resort just north of Quebec City, to Resorts of the Canadian Rockies.

Other major deals would soon follow. In June 1999, Canadian Hotel Income Properties (CHIP), a real estate investment trust (REIT), received an hostile takeover bid from another REIT, Royal Host, which has an asset base of C$300 million, which includes 3,500 rooms at 33 hotels. CHIP, Canada's first hotel REIT, owns and operates nearly 8,000 rooms at 36 hotels across Canada. Participating with Royal Host in its bid is Westmont Corp., which stands to gain a few more hotels for its new Canadian operations.

Meanwhile, activity also is occurring in other niche sectors of Canada's hospitality industry. In mid-1998, Canada's Vinings

Franchise Systems and Atlanta-based U.S. Franchise Systems, reached an agreement to bring the Microtel brand concept to Canada. Microtel Inns & Suites is a growing, franchised chain of newly constructed budget and economy hotels.

Continuing this trend to bring quality budget lodging to Canada, Cendant Corp.'s Knights Franchise Systems, Inc. signed its first international master franchise agreement for the development of Knights Inn brand hotels in Canada with AFM Hospitality of Toronto. AFM, which already holds the master franchise for Cendant's Ramada and Howard Johnson brands in Canada, expects to add more than 100 Knights Inns during the next five years, recently opening its first in Niagara Falls, Ontario. AFM also recently signed a deal with Seattle-based AST Brands LLC to bring the Aston brand to Canada.

Largely attributed to Canadian "snowbirds" escaping the winter for a warm-weather holiday in the U.S. or Caribbean, Canada has long suffered a tourism trade deficit. But with tourism spending growth rate within Canada expected to top 4% annually coupled with a declining rate of growth in tourism spending by Canadians abroad, a trade balance is projected within two to three years.

Indeed, this new strength in the hospitality sector has not been lost on the industry's major players in Canada, where consolidation is not only the major trend in the industry, but also the driving force behind change as we enter the new millennium.

The Risks in Computerization and Information Management

Hotel managers awakened in the early morning hours to news of an earthquake, fire or explosion are unlikely to think first of saving the hotel's AS400 information system or retrieving computer data tapes from off-site locations. Evacuating guests and employees is paramount. Disaster plans put people first. Nevertheless, loss of a property's information technology (IT) functions can plunge any company into operational disarray, triggering revenue losses and negative publicity that may take years to overcome. Technology systems rendered inoperable in one location can ripple through an entire hotel organization, forcing the company to fall back on manual operations. Reservations, property management and communications systems must be quickly replaced and guest data recovered to avoid major losses.

A case in point involved the bombing of New York's World Trade Centre in 1993. The terrorist act inflicted physical damage to a large area of downtown Manhattan, including an adjacent hotel. Although the hotel was evacuated in less than fifteen minutes with no fatalities, the telephone and computer system was damaged. The hotel could not account for guests and employees. Communications failures prevented management from communicating with emergency services.

The loss of heat could have caused further damage to existing systems from the bursting of frozen water pipes. The hotel's experience points to one of the key elements in a technology disaster recovery plan-maintaining critical operational and financial data at an off-site storage facility. Following a disaster, off-site facilities that maintain reservation and accounting information would be available immediately for retrieval of in-house guest records, financial documents, guest history and sales information, minimizing a disaster's effect on a hotel's data and information.

Prompted by insurance companies or experience, most companies have addressed the need for a disaster recovery plan (DRP), if not put one in place. Few, however, create and maintain written plans on IT disaster recovery. In a survey conducted by Comdisco, Inc., one of the largest disaster recovery companies, it was estimated that only 45 percent of companies maintain a formal plan in the event of computer disruption.

The survey addressed the level of corporate readiness for disaster recovery, concluding that only 12 percent of enterprises have an effective disaster recovery plan. Another 6 percent were partially prepared. Fully 82 percent of companies were ineffectively prepared for a technology disaster. The survey measured: 1) data centers, 2) local area networks, and 3) enterprise wide area networks. While the survey itself was cross-industry, hospitality companies rely heavily on all three of the technology components measured. A disaster recovery plan specifically addressing technology is essential to any hotel's risk management programs.

Threats to Technology Systems

One of the most destructive events for hospitality companies occurred in September 1992 as Hurricane Iniki unleashed winds up to 200 miles per hour on the Island of Kauai, Hawaii. The damage amounted to $1.6 billion and resulted in 85 percent of the island's hotel rooms shutting down for at least two months. With 30-foot waves and complete power outages, all hotel technology systems on the island were lost.

Particularly in areas with potential for destructive weather, the need for disaster recovery and off-site back up systems cannot be overstated. Hotel properties without technology disaster recovery plans may be closed for much longer periods of time than other companies.

Of the 320 technology recoveries supported by Comdisco since 1985, hardware failure was the largest cause at 24 percent, followed by hurricanes and power outages at 16 percent each, and floods accounting for another 15 percent. The seeds of major technology failures may occur within the systems themselves. One of the largest providers of global distribution of airline and hotel reservations experienced an outage in mid-1998 due to a software error, resulting in the complete cessation of new reservations bookings for more than five hours. An outage on a system that processes an hourly average of 45,000 airline and hotel reservations can cause major service disruptions and customer dissatisfaction.

Even a supplier with a system that is 99.9 percent reliable must expect and plan for a system failure. Senior management may be unaware of the need to maintain detailed back-up plans for systems and data. Only a select few in the if department may consider systems recovery as a primary function in the event of a disaster.

Almost all hospitality companies have one main database for reservations and guest history. Both are at risk if a disaster occurs. In addition, the industry's reliance on technology and communication creates several less traditional risks.

The global distribution system, the importance of customer data, productivity heavily reliant on terminals and information, and the long-term effect on loyalty of a single negative experience, are additional risks particularly present in the hospitality industry. In addition, companies are racing to build information about customer and spending patterns, investing millions of dollars in systems to institutionalize this knowledge. Loss of these systems and databases is analogous to organizational memory' loss. While rebuilding physical property may take several years, guest loyalty and behavioral history' may often require more time and money.

Disaster Categories

320 Recoveries Supported

Hardware Problems	24%
Power Outage	16%
Hurricane	16%
Flood	15%
Miscellaneous	12%
Fire / Explosion	7%
Bomb	5%
Earthquake	5%

Source: Comdisco

Creating a Disaster Recovery Plan

Clearly, the development of a technology disaster recovery' plan is an essential part of any company/s risk management program. Its development and documentation at a minimum will require the following steps:

Take an Inventory: Include items critical to the business, including the reservation system, database and the systems that support it. Telecommunications (dial-up lines, frame relay, dedicated lines and the Internet) can be included as support systems.

Assess Unavailability: Assess what will occur if critical systems are absent over specific periods of time. Ask key questions for each system. What foreseeable impact exists if accounting functionality is down, for example, or the property management system applications are non-responsive? Determine the maximum amount of downtime for these critical items before there will be a significant impact on the business.

Identify Alternatives: Identify disaster recovery alternatives for critical functions. Hospitality companies might decide that a "hot site" is a reasonable alternative with the loss of a reservation system. A hot site is a computer and data processing centre with computers in place and waiting to be used by a company experiencing a disaster. Most hot sites are permanent facilities where the company can recreate its computing environment.

Determine Alternative Requirements: Identify what is needed for an alternative to be implemented. Minimum requirements may involve telecommunications with certain bandwidths or dial-up lines. A specified level of power redundancy may be required for servers. Agreements with hardware vendors or vendors who provide disaster recovery sites may also be an option.

Identify Costs: Gain an understanding of the total cost for each alternative. Examples of common costs include arranging hardware agreements with vendors or the cost of having a disaster recovery site available for use. Installation fees, purchase of redundant telecommunications, and the purchase of upgrading telecommunications (i.e., increasing bandwidth) are other common costs. Some hospitality companies may have additional costs relating to reservation system development time as a minimum alternative requirement.

Estimate the Recovery Period: Estimate the amount of time until the critical systems become available. Each alternative should have a specified recovery period.

Define the Limitations: Determine the limitations of each system back-up or alternative, including vendor agreements or hot sites. The plan needs to address questions of hardware replacement, especially if it is rare, discontinued, or a lag time exists between the purchase order and its delivery. The cost of an alternative or the length of time until availability may also be limitations.

Determine the Benefits: Weigh the benefits of each alternative. Use the benefits of a faster recovery in the event of a disaster as a competitive advantage.

Test the Plan Annually: Document the test and test results as a best practice to provide a record of any problems encountered and their resolution.

IT Training in Disaster Recovery: Provide proper training of IT personnel for implementation of the disaster recovery plan.

When a disaster or hardware failure does occur, planning rigor will make all the difference in the speed of recovery. A completed disaster recovery plan for technology systems allows companies to realize large returns on a relatively small investment-minimizing what may otherwise be an unnecessary and costly outcome of disasters.

Hotel Companies Plan Future Strategies after Consolidation

The pace of consolidation within the global hotel industry has quickened in the last year. The resulting organisations are now concentrating their resources on how to develop and add further value to their existing and inherited brands. The strategies of Bass Hotels and Resorts, Starwood Lodging and Patriot American Hospitality illustrate the priority that hotel companies give to increasing brand awareness in a competitive marketplace.

Bass Hotels and Resorts

At a recent conference in New Orleans, it was confirmed that Bass Hotels and Resorts (BHR) will continue to focus on brand preference and the distribution of each chain in its relevant market. BHR is also planning a significant investment and aggressive expansion. Some US$1 billion is destined for the Inter-Continental brand, whilst increased advertising and promotion of loyalty schemes will enhance the market's awareness of the company 5 other brands, in particular Holiday Inn Express and Staybridge Suites. The company is also focusing on boosting its presence in the Middle East with several major projects under construction in Egypt, further expansion in Saudi Arabia, and a number of developments in Lebanon and Jordan.

Starwood Lodging

Following the acquisition of Sheraton and Westin, Starwood has invested US$400 million in its portfolio. During the first half of 1998, 49 management agreements were signed with a further 20 scheduled for the latter part of the year. Twenty-two hotels have been converted to the Westin or Four Points brands. For the new brand, sites under construction include five in North America, three in New York, one in Seattle and one in San Francisco.

Starwood also announced that it will be combining its REIT and Starwood Hotels and Resorts to create a single C-corp with the REIT as a subsidiary. This allows the corporation to work around the change in federal law that precludes "paired share" REITs from growing through future asset acquisitions.

Patriot American Hospitality

During the third quarter of 1998, 19 hotels were converted to the Wyndham brand, and Patriot predicts that the brand will have grown from 78 units at the beginning of the year to 185 owned or managed properties by December 1998. During the second quarter, nine former Grand Heritage hotels were repositioned as part of the Wyndham Grand Heritage brand.

In the meantime, the luxury hotel division, which currently consists of 11 properties, will be branded Grand Bay Hotels and Resorts. The existing Carefree Resorts, Grand Bay Hotels and Golden Door Spa will he folded into this new operation. The roll-out of this brand will be limited to between 25 and 30 hotels in the next five years to maintain the exclusivity of the product.

Gambling in the Las Vegas

Whilst the rest of the world looks cautiously to the future and development plans are put on hold or scaled down, Las Vegas is once again breaking the mold.

During the next two and a half years, 20,000 new rooms will be added. A large percentage of these are in the form of "mega-hotels" such as Hilton's "Paris' property with replicas of the Eiffel Tower and Arc de Triomphe. The scale of this new building boom is significant in itself, but the fact that it is occurring at a time of such global economic uncertainty, has raised questions about the scale of development.

There is also the added worry that the local hotel market has softened somewhat, with occupancy rates now at 86 percent compared with more than 90 percent two years ago. These levels are, of course, still extremely high, but when companies operate on the assumption of full capacity it becomes a significant drop. The turmoil in the Asian market is also taking its toll, especially with the intentional high rolling gamblers. In addition, Las Vegas 10 years ago had a monopoly in legalised gambling; today additional jurisdictions have legalised gambling. The competition is getting tougher. In an attempt to attract more families to Las Vegas in the early years of this decade, the city introduced Disney-style entertainment, but gambling and other forms of themed entertainment do not always combine well and the results have been somewhat mixed.

...: and for the rest of the world?

In spite of concerns over current and future trading conditions, many hotel companies are considering further investment and expansion across the world. Recent announcements include.

Following a 22 percent increase in profit for the six months to June 1998, U.K.-based Millennium & Copthorne Hotels has announced expansion plans. These are said to include continental Europe and gateway cities in the United States, such as Chicago, Los Angeles, Washington DC, Dallas and Atlanta.

Paris-based Accor SA is undergoing an aggressive expansion plan in Europe and South America. In Poland, the company is seeking to establish subsidiaries and joint venture partners to assist them in their development plan in central Europe. There are to be over 25 Ibis properties within the next two years. The company hopes to establish a network of over 30 Etap budget hotels during the next five years. In Brazil, Accor aims to have developed 5,500 rooms in 40 cities by the year 2002 with an initial investment of US$21 million.

Accor is also continuing its interest in expanding into Asia. Speculation continues over their interest in bidding for Century

International. It has been reported in the French press that Accor is interested in expanding via the partial acquisition of Hong Kong-based Regal Hotels International. For the first nine months of 1998, Starwood announced a 7 percent increase in revenue per available room (RevPar) for their owned hotels worldwide, with increases in Europe, Latin America and North America of 14 percent, 8 percent and 6 percent respectively.

This resulted in a 14 percent increase in EBITDA. The casino operation faired equally well with an increase in revenues of 28 percent. Starwood's development plans not only include the hotels division, but also the casino group. By the year 2000 there will be a Caesar's riverboat in Indiana, USA with 90,000 square feet of casino space and a 500-room hotel. A joint venture in Johannesburg, South Africa with Guateng will create 75,000 square feet of casino space and a 200-room hotel.

For the lodging brands of Marriott International in the United States for quarter three, RevPar grew by 5 percent compared with the previous year. Results for the international properties were moderately lower in 1998 due to the difficult trading conditions in the Asia-Pacific region.

This dip was partially offset by profit growth in Europe, the Middle East and Latin America. However, the company expects to increase its portfolio by more than 150,000 rooms during the next five years, 30,000 of which are to open in 1998 within 200 hotels.

Utilising US$500 million of equity, Swissotel is eager to increase its current portfolio of 24 hotels to 60 properties by the year 2000. Currently the portfolio covers five continents with hotels concentrated in the main business centres and resort areas. For the future, Swissotel is seeking a presence in Los Angeles, San Francisco, Miami, London, Paris, Singapore, Hong Kong and Tokyo.

One may be surprised to learn that hotel companies are seeking developments in Asia, but Swissotel management reportedly believes that the economic situation in that region provides a good opportunity for growth.

In Jericho Peace Prevails on the Gaming Tables

The Oasis Casino opened in September 1998 and is situated in the Jordan valley, close to the ancient town of Jericho. Operated by Casinos Austria, the recently opened US$150 million Oasis has been attracting large numbers of Israelis. According to reports, in the first weeks after opening, at least 1,000 people each day could be seen waiting to enter the casino, which had already reached capacity. Frustrated crowds even tried to enter the premises through the staff entrance to gain a chance to try their luck at one of the 45 gambling tables and 220 slot machines.

This dramatic exposure of frustrated demand has spurred Israeli politicians to revive a governmental committee, which was appointed by late Prime Minister Yitzhak Rabin, to establish two casinos in Israel on a trial basis. The Gavish Committee has previously had to deliberate over the possible pros and cons of developing a casino in the highly popular Red Sea destination of Eilat.

The initial decision on opening a casino was postponed but remains eagerly awaited by local hotel operators who are expecting strong increases in demand from visiting gamblers. The Oasis Casino is expected to generate positive side effects for the local economy, supporting the 30,000 population resident in Jericho.

The casino employs some 1,000 locals, and the economic spillover from the traffic created by gamblers who come from Jerusalem and even as far as Tel Aviv is having a positive effect on the local population's attitude towards the casino. Spending in Jericho has increased considerably, which in turn has had a positive impact on a number of critics who had previously rallied against the casino prior to its opening.

U.K. Travel Industry Consolidation to Set a Global Trend

Consolidation of the U.K. travel industry has progressed at a rapid pace during the past six months. The greatest level of activity has been witnessed by the major players, as they aim to fight off competition by increasing market share and the number of distribution channels in existing markets, or obtain footholds in new markets.

Some examples of major deals in recent months include:

- Acquisition of Unijet and Hayes & Jarvis by First Choice for £134 million in June 1998;
- Purchase of Direct Holidays by Airtours in July 1998 for £80.7 million;
- Acquisition of Crystal Holidays by Thomson for £66.2 million in August 1998; and
- Announcement of the merger between Thomas Cook and U.S.-based Carlson in October 1998, which, if approved by the Monopolies and Mergers Commission, would create one of the world's largest leisure travel companies.

The high level of activity by the leading U.K. tour operators has forced other companies to take a closer look at their distribution channels. In October 1998, First Choice, Britain's third largest tour operator, unveiled its new distribution strategy. In addition to purchasing retail travel agent Bakers Dolphin for £12 million and acquiring minority stakes in the regional chains Hays Travel and Holiday Express, it is also planning to open 533 new shops within the next two years.

Simultaneously, First Choice is buying a 25 percent stake in Holiday Hypermarkets. Holiday Hypermarkets is a pioneering new concept in retail travel, and it is estimated that the 10,000 square foot shops will generate fifteen times the number of bookings of an ordinary travel shop.

At the same time, U.K. companies have begun to diversify geographically through acquisitions in Northern Europe and North America. In October 1998, Airtours announced the acquisition of US-based tour operator Vacation Express for US$24.3 million. In Europe, operators are very keen to gain a foothold in Europe's largest outbound market, Germany.

Airtours was the first U.K. tour operator to gain entry, with the purchase of a 29 percent stake in Frosch Touristik (FTi) and a further option to purchase the remainder in 2002. Thomson is also pursuing foreign expansion, having almost reached its maximum allowable market share in the United Kingdom. Under

U.K. law more than 25 percent market share would technically make it a monopoly and consequently in breach of the rules of the Monopolies and Mergers Commission. According to Travel Industry Digest, Thomson is reportedly believed to lie interested in a potential alliance with Neckermann, Germany's second largest tour operator.

The current activity from the major U.K. tour operators is likely to continue, as they remain eager to gain a foothold in foreign markets. The Thomas Cook/Carlson deal indicates activity will most likely move away from takeovers into formal alliances and share swaps as a means of consolidation..

3

Hotel Financial Automation

Introduction

When you stayed in that luxury hotel during your last vacation, did you check what your neighbour paid for her room? If she were a business visitor, she could have paid well above $300 for the same room that you paid $180. It is also possible that she paid $120 provided she planned well in advance and managed to get that "better" deal which was elusive to you. So why do hotels charge different customers different rates for the same type of room? Such differences are the result of an increasingly common strategy to maximize revenue (and profits) in the Hotel industry–a practice referred to as Revenue or Yield Management.

Revenue Management (RM) is a scientific technique that combines Operations Research, Statistics and Customer Relationship Management (CRM) and categorizes customers into price bands, based on various services. Statistical analysis of past data helps in forecasting demand and establishing the appropriate price bands. Applied correctly, Revenue Management helps hotels expand market size and increase revenues. Some industry practitioners also refer to RM as the art of selling the right room to the right customer at the right time and for the right price.

To understand the need for an RM system, let us take the following two examples. At the peak of the SARS epidemic in Canada, a resort experienced a 25% drop in number of visitors. Amazingly, this resort managed to limit decline in revenue to a bare 3%. During economic depression, a travel management company reduced its marketing budget by half, but still managed a revenue increase of 6%. How were these successes possible? The answer to both of these questions lies with the implementation of Revenue Management strategy.

Why Revenue Management?

- *Segmented Market:* Hotels typically segment their market (customer base) into a set of categories based on the price each category is willing to pay. Typical categories include the business traveler and the vacation traveler. Because demand patterns for each of these categories may vary significantly, hotels find it difficult to satisfy all of the demand simultaneously. A good example is the comparison between the time-conscious business executive and the price-sensitive vacation customer. The former is willing to pay a higher price in exchange for flexibility of being able to book a room at the last minute while the latter is willing to give up some flexibility for the sake of a more inexpensive room. RM tries to maximize revenues by managing the trade-off between a low occupancy and higher room rate scenario (business customers) versus a high occupancy and lower room rate (vacation customers). Such a strategy allows hotels to fill rooms that would otherwise have been empty.
- *Fixed Capacity*: A hotel's capacity is relatively fixed-it is nearly impossible to add or remove rooms based on fluctuations in demand. If at all hotel capacity were flexible, there would be no need to manage capacity.
- *Perishable Inventory*: In the hotel industry, hotel rooms are the inventory. A hotel room that remains unoccupied for a night loses all its value for that night. This inventory cannot be stored and is lost forever. Because RM tries to manage demand instead of supply, it proves to be good business sense for the hotel.
- *Low Marginal Cost*: The fixed cost of adding a room in a hotel is heavily capital intensive. However, once the hotel manages to cover its initial fixed costs, the cost of serving an additional customer is low enough that the hotel can

sell the room at a lower margin if it wishes. Such a strategy will obviously need to be balanced by one that also seeks to sell the room(s) at higher margins. Thus, the high fixed cost/low marginal cost nature of the business makes price differentiation a necessity-something that is made possible by application of RM.

- *Advanced Sales*: More often than not, requests for bookings start early. Therefore, hotels have enough leeway to adjust room prices based on the variation between realized bookings and expected demand. If all hotel rooms are sold at the same time, the hotel does not have the flexibility to adjust prices upward if demand picks up later. The trade-off occurs when a manager is faced with the option of accepting an early reservation from a customer who wants a low price, or waiting to see if a higher paying customer will eventually show up...
- *Demand Fluctuations*: Demand for hotel rooms is characterized by crests and troughs, which the hotel factors in during the room pricing process. In peak season, the hotel can increase its revenues by raising room prices, while during lean seasons it can increase its utilization rate by lowering prices. Past data will offer the manager a way to forecast when these periods of high and low demand may occur. Unfortunately, it is very difficult to predict the actual demand with a high degree of certainty.

Therefore, the most critical challenge facing the hotel industry is predicting potential capacity, and developing a pricing strategy that will encourage maximum capacity and revenue. Revenue Management is the most effective technique to solve this challenge, similar to aggregate and hierarchical production planning techniques often employed in the manufacturing industry. Revenue Management is based on complex optimization methodologies developed from advanced statistical and analytical models.

In order to arrive at a solution, managers need to evaluate several millions of decisions, which requires a significant investment of skills, hardware and time. Many RM practitioners prefer to breakdown the actual business scenario into four sub-problems, and then identify an individual solution to some or all of these sub-problems. This would significantly reduce the number of potential non-optimal decisions thereby providing fewer choices, leading to quicker results.

These four sub-problems are:

(a) Market segment identification,

(b) Forecasting and Pricing,

(c) Inventory allocation, and

(d) Overbooking.

How does it all Work?

Market Segment Identification

The first and foremost step in a hotel RM system is the identification of the various market segments for the hotel room, followed by implementation of a differential pricing scheme. The objective in front of the hotel is the expansion of its market and in motivating the customer to pay more than he/she will usually spend. It is further observed that customers in the business class segment are less sensitive to higher prices as opposed to those in the vacation segment. An RM system helps hotels create additional price-points by building physical and logical fences around the different market segments, as shown in the table below.

CHARACTERISTICS	HIGHER PRICE	LOWER PRICE
Physical Fences		
View	Pool view, ocean view, hill view	Non-scenic view
Size	Bigger room with more facilities and gadgets	Smaller rooms with fewer facilities
Temporal	Weekday bookings	Weekend bookings
Logical Fences		
Length of Stay	Short stay. Often one or two days	Longer stay. One night revenue can spoil three nights revenue when demand is high
Flexibility	Cancellations and rescheduling are allowed at a low penalty	High penalty for cancellation and schedule changes
Time of Purchase	Bookings are made very close to date of check-in	Bookings are made quite early
Privileges	Are rewarded loyalty privileges either as free services or free stay vouchers	No privileges
Size of Business Provided	Corporate business customers booking frequently	Self funding vacationers booking rarely
Point of Sale	Physical delivery and confirmations	By email or phone

Demand Forecasting

The next step in an RM process is forecasting demand and pricing of the different market segments. Pricing and demand are inter-related and need to be coordinated. In the hotel industry, demand for a room is cyclic in nature (day of a week, months of a year) and follows a trend (demand growth due to economic growth). These forecasts are seldom precise but provide the decision-maker with an approximate set of inputs that are used in the planning process. RM models help pinpoint demand by minimizing uncertainty and producing the best possible forecast.

Allocation

The next important step in a RM process is the allocation of inventory (hotel rooms) among different market segments. The ratio of discounted versus full priced rooms is not fixed during the reservation period; rather, it is "tweaked" appropriately as the date of stay approaches. The opportunity cost of selling a discounted room instead of a full priced one has to be measured in order to make the best decision. Thus, when a customer approaches the hotel for a discounted price, the manager needs to evaluate this scenario with the expected revenue from another customer who might come at a later date, willing to pay a higher price for the same room. The manager would accept the request only if the discounted price now is more than the expected price at which the room might be booked by the second customer. The key word here is "expected". RM systems use complicated mathematical algorithms to arrive at this decision using techniques such as Littlewoods and Expectation Maximization, referred to as the EM algorithm.

To explain these techniques, let us consider a simple two class scenario. A hotel has two price categories of rooms, say $60 and $100. Since the pricing is different for the two rooms, these rooms are each targeted at a different customer set. Based on the historical preference pattern of customers in each segment, it would be possible to estimate the number of customers who would be willing to buy these rooms at the given price, with a reasonable "variance". The term variance refers to a tolerance level. For example, an average 50 customers may be willing to pay $100 for some rooms, but it could also mean that the actual number of customers who turn up for the $100 room could be 60 (or even 40) with some probability, or 80 (or 30) with a lesser probability. In statistical terms, this sort of pattern for the different customer segments is said to mimic a normal distribution.

Using the past data and applying statistical know-how, we can actually estimate an "expectation" of revenue by quantifying the probability of a specific demand value and the actual revenue. In the same example, let us assume that this hotel has 100 rooms, which are similar, but priced at the time of booking. If the booking is done fairly closely to the actual date of stay, the customers may need to pay $100, whereas, they might have paid only $60 had they booked in advance. Remember that, on an average, 50 persons are willing to pay $100 for this room. Obviously, many more than 50 (say, 120) are willing to $60 for the same room. We can use the Littlewoods rule to actually estimate the number of rooms that must be protected for those customers who are willing to pay $100. If we protect too many rooms, some rooms may go vacant thereby resulting in a loss of potential revenue of at least $60 per room. On the other hand if we protect too few rooms for $100 customers, we lose the opportunity of $40 per room on that number of rooms. The Littlewoods rule guides us to arrive at an optimal number of rooms that would maximize the expectation of revenues.

Overbooking

Overbooking is the practice of intentionally selling more rooms than are available in order to offset the effect of cancellations and no-shows. Studies estimate that although a hotel is fully booked, about 5-8% of the rooms are vacant on any given date. Poor overbooking decisions can prove to be very expensive for the hotel. In the short run, it is only a loss of room revenue, but over the long-term, casualties may include decreased customer loyalty, loss of hotel reputation, etc. American Airlines developed an optimization model that maximizes net revenues associated with overbooking decisions for the airline industry.

To illustrate the overbooking model developed by the American Airlines, let us consider a B757 jet flying from Chicago to Boston.

The aircraft has about 180 seats. Based on the past travel pattern, it is observed that an average of 5% (or nine passengers) do not turn up at the time of boarding the flight. If the airlines book all seats for this leg, it is likely to fly with only 171 occupied seats. However it does not mean that it never flies with 172 or more (even 180) seats occupied. There is a lesser chance of the flight flying with 172 passengers, an even lesser chance of it flying with 175 and a miniscule chance of it flying with all 180 passengers. Therefore, if we book 181 passengers instead of 180, we are likely to end up with only 173 passengers (and almost always with lesser than 180 passengers). In an odd event of exactly 181 passengers reporting, the airline would need to bump one passenger. IATA has defined rules to compensate bumped passengers. If we can quantify all costs (including the cost of lost goodwill), the expected revenue would be the revenue from 181 passengers minus the expected cost of compensating the one additional passenger at that odd chance. Since the probability of exactly 181 passengers turning up is so low, the revenue from that additional passenger generally compensates more than the expected cost. For this example, the optimal number of passengers that can be booked would be 186 as illustrated in the figure below.

This model can be directly applied to the hotel industry as well. The driving force behind the model is the evaluation of the trade-off between additional revenue accrued by selling an already-reserved room versus the downside from doing so. It has been found that net revenue increases with overbooking until the point where the downside from overbooking a room exceeds customer revenues. Beyond that point, the negative impact of overbooking increases rapidly because fewer and fewer customers appreciate being turned away.

Challenges

It is quite clear that while an RM system can guarantee increased revenues, it can be quite complicated to design and requires high levels of expertise for implementation. Some of the challenges facing hotels in the implementation of a robust and accurate RM system include:

- Measuring performance of an RM system is a major issue. Occupancy rates and yield are measures that are affected by external competition. An ideal measurement can be done using an opportunity model that indicates where the hotel stands in comparison to its maximum and
- Differential pricing is here to stay-customers seem resigned to the fact that hotels charge different prices for the same room. However, some customers do not like this practice and penalize the hotel by not becoming a patron. Therefore, in a fiercely competitive environment where quality of service is the key to success, RM may not work. In evaluating the efficiency of a RM system, the trade-off between generating short-term profits and creating long-term customer loyalty and "mindshare" needs to be studied carefully.
- From an operational point of view, RM can impact the motivational level of the employees. In many cases, RM takes much of the guess work out of employees, thereby reducing their decision-making responsibilities. Sometimes, employees taking reservations are paid a percentage of the sales they make, motivating them to make group bookings, which in turn may be contradictory with the objectives of an RM system.

Conclusion

As part of ongoing changes in the industry, companies throughout the entire hospitality spectrum are placing a strong emphasis on implementing major operational changes.

Beyond recognizing that meaningful cost reductions must be achieved without compromising safety, capacity and service levels, they are also looking at reducing costs by increasing flexibility and improving asset utilization through an RM strategy.

In doing so, they continue to reassess their true core competencies, and are looking to outsource many of these processes, as they look to optimize business efficiencies and increase profitability.

Budgeting Hospitality Industry

Policy Statement

The capital improvements program includes all capital projects, regardless of size, financed with state and University funds, and all departmentally funded projects exceeding $100,000 (see the Special Situations section for information on projects less than $100,000). The capital improvements program is an ongoing process that includes:

- Assessing capital needs, opportunities and resources
- Ensuring that potential projects conform with academic priorities & investment strategies
- Establishing priorities for project funding.

Provosts, Chancellors and Vice-Presidents submit their capital improvement needs for review by the Capital Improvements Advisory Committee which recommends systemwide priorities to the Senior Officers of the University. The President submits the capital budget to the Regents.

Exclusions

Purchases of free-standing instructional and research equipment, even those large enough to be categorized as a "capital expense", should be funded through the operating budget, and should not be submitted to the capital budgeting process. None of the funding sources available for allocation through the capital budget are available for free-standing equipment purchases.

Special Situations

Self-funded projects of less than $100,000 do not require individual approval by the Regents, and are, therefore, excluded from the capital budget process. These projects are handled as follows:

1. Projects are initiated by submitting a Form 1395 request to Capital Planning and Project Management with the dean's sign-off that the proposed project:
   * Conforms with academic priorities of the University

   * Has adequate funding identified

2. Projects are briefly reviewed to ensure that the proposed project:
   * Is within a facility worth investment
   * Will not significantly increase the cost of maintaining and operating the facility
   * Addresses code compliance issues
   * Causes no negative impact on adjacent space/facilities
   * Conforms with campus master planning principles
3. Projects that meet the preceding criteria will be scheduled for implementation immediately. Projects that do not appear to satisfy all of these criteria will be referred to the CIAC for review and recommendation, and to the Senior Officers for concurrence.
4. If during the planning and design stage the cost of a project increases beyond the $100,000 threshold, the project will be considered in the next capital budgeting cycle, or if the need is urgent, it may be handled as an amendment to the capital budget, requiring the review and recommendation of the CIAC, the concurrence of the Senior Officers, and the approval of the Regents.

Purchases of free-standing instructional and research equipment, even those large enough to be categorized as a "capital expense", should be funded through the operating budget, and should not be submitted to the capital budgeting process. None of the funding sources available for allocation through the capital budget are available for free-standing equipment purchases.

However, if the equipment purchases require adjustments to building systems (examples: expanded electrical capacity, HVAC modification) or remodelling of space, those facility improvements should be submitted to the capital budgeting process in accordance with the definitions regarding project size and funding source contained in Section C. A department purchasing equipment which requires building adjustments must either invest departmental funds to achieve those modifications, or must request central funds through the capital budgeting process. If the purchase of equipment represents a high programmatic priority, the priorities for distributing capital resources may be influenced.

Reason for Policy

To assist the President in preparing the capital budget and capital improvements program. To facilitate informed investment decisions and promote effective management of existing capital assets.

Submitting a Project for the Capital Budget

Procedure

Types of Projects

All projects meeting the following definitions must be submitted to the capital budgeting process:

- Projects requesting central or state funding, regardless of size. Central and state funding sources include fire and life safety, ADA improved access, hazardous materials abatement, repair and replacement, program accommodation remodelling, internal loans, central reserves, University bonds and state bonds.
- Self-funded projects which exceed $100,000. Self-funding sources include departmental funds (O&M, ISO, ICR, gifts and grants) and fees collected by self-supported auxiliary services.

Academic units should submit only projects related to their programmatic needs. Projects that relate exclusively to fire and life safety, improved access, hazardous material abatement, or repair and replacement, should be referred to the units, listed below, that are responsible for addressing those needs.

Type of Improvement-Responsible Unit

Fire and Life Safety-University Building Official.

ADA access-Facilities Management TC Campus FM or Plant Services on other campuses. Hazardous material-Environmental

Health and Safety / TC abatement Campus and air quality FM or Plant Services on other campuses. Repair and replacement-Facilities Management on TC Campus FM or Plant Services on other campuses.

Submitting A Project

Submit capital projects to the capital budgeting process in the following manner:

- Departments identify a capital need, complete a project identification form, and submit it to the College or Resource Responsibility Center (RRC). Attach a copy of the project identification form.
- Colleges/RRCs review the requested capital improvement, assign a priority ranking to the request, and submit it to the Provost/Chancellor/Vice President.
- Provosts/Chancellors/Vice Presidents review the requested capital improvement, assign a preliminary priority ranking to the request, submit it to the Office of Budget and Finance, and present it to the Capital Improvements Advisory Committee (CIAC) budget hearings.

Project Identification Form

A project identification form must be submitted for all projects proposed for the period, including projects which were previously submitted and incorporated into the Capital Improvements Program. Each annual capital budget and capital improvements program is treated as a new undertaking, and confirmation of each project and its priority ranking is required if it is to remain in the capital improvements program.

Project identification forms for projects included in the current capital improvements program are being returned to the Provosts, Chancellors, and Vice Presidents with instructions. Persons proposing those projects may obtain the forms from their Provost, Chancellor, or Vice President in order to improve the project information. If there are no changes, simply resubmit the sheets.

Project Identification Forms must be submitted by Oct. 31, 1996 CAPITAL BUDGET

To be considered for inclusion in the Capital Budget, the following conditions must be satisfied:

- Proposed construction projects must have a comprehensive cost estimate prepared by or under the direction of Capital Planning and Project Management. Proposed land or facility acquisitions must have an appraisal approved by the Real Estate Office.
- Proposed projects must have funding available, or have funding contingent upon a pending grant application or private gifts from an active fund raising campaign.

Unless both of these conditions are satisfied, the project will not be included in the Capital Budget, but will instead be placed in a future fiscal year of the capital improvements program.

Prior to Regents' approval of the capital budget, the Office of Budget and Finance will verify the availability of funding for projects which are dependent upon State and University funds. Departments and auxiliaries will be asked to verify the availability of funding for projects to be financed with departmental funds or with fees collected by self-supported auxiliaries by providing a CUFS account number, or by identifying a Foundation account, a grant application, or a fund raising effort.

Verification of funding must be received annually by April 1.

Projects must be identified during the annual budgeting process if they are to be considered for inclusion in the Capital Budget. Projects which are not identified at this time will be deferred to next year's budgeting cycle. Only in extraordinary circumstances will projects be considered as amendments to the approved capital budget during the course of the year. Budget amendments require special review and recommendation by the CIAC, concurrence by the Senior Officers, and approval by the Board of Regents. Implementation of a project cannot proceed until it has been included in the capital budget.

Equipment Purchases

Purchases of free-standing instructional and research equipment, even those large enough to be categorized as a "capital expense", should be funded through the operating budget, and should not be submitted to the capital budgeting process. None of the funding sources available for allocation through the capital budget are available for free-standing equipment purchases.

However, if the equipment purchases being considered will require adjustments to building systems (examples: expanded electrical capacity, HVAC modification) or remodelling of space, those facility improvements should be submitted to the capital budgeting process in accordance with the definitions regarding project size and funding source described at the beginning of this procedure. A department purchasing equipment which requires building adjustments must either invest departmental funds to achieve those modifications, or must request central funds through the capital budgeting process. If the purchase of equipment represents a high programmatic priority, the priorities for distributing capital resources may be influenced.

Discussion Issues and Derivations

Working Capital, Net Working Capital and Non-Cash Working Capital

Working capital is sometimes used to refer only to current assets, while net working capital is defined to be the difference between current assets and current liabilities. Non-cash working capital looks at the difference between non-cash current assets and current liabilities.

In investment analysis, increases in working capital are viewed as cash outflows, because cash tied up in working capital cannot be used elsewhere in the business and does not earn returns. It is the "does not earn returns" component of this definition that would lead us to look at non-cash working capital. Firms with significant cash balances today, especially in the US, earn market returns on their cash (by investing in at least T.Bills). Thus, the cash is productive and changes in the cash should not affect our cash flows.

To the degree that cash cannot be invested to earn market returns, and is needed for day-to-day operations, it is appropriate to look at changes in net working capital, with cash included.

Operating versus Capital Expenditures

Accountants draw a distinction between expenditures that yield benefits only in the immediate period or periods (such as labour and material for a manufacturing firm) and those that yield benefits over multiple periods (such as land, buildings and long-lived plant). The former are called operating expenses and are subtracted from revenues in computing the accounting income, while the latter are capital expenditures and are not subtracted from revenues in the period that they are made. Instead, the expenditure is spread over multiple periods and deducted as an expense in each period-these expenses are called depreciation (if the asset is a tangible asset like a building) or amortization (if the asset is an intangible asset like a patent or a trade mark).

While the capital expenditures made at the beginning of a project are often the largest and most prominent, many projects require capital expenditures during their lifetime. These capital expenditures will reduce the cash available in each of these periods.

Depreciation, Amortization and Other Non-cash Charges

The distinction that accountants draw between operating and capital expenses leads to a number of accounting expenses, such as depreciation and amortization, which are not cash expenses. These non-cash expenses, while depressing accounting income, do not reduce cash flows. In fact, they can have a significant positive impact on cash flows, if they affect the tax liability of the firm. Some non-cash charges reduce the taxable income and the taxes paid by a business. The most important of such charges is depreciation, which, while reducing taxable and net income, does not cause a cash outflow. Consequently, depreciation is added back to net income to arrive at the cash flows on a project. For projects that generate large depreciation charges, a significant portion of the cash flows can be attributed to the tax benefits of depreciation, which can be written as follows

Tax Benefit of Depreciation = Depreciation * Marginal Tax Rate

While depreciation is similar to other tax deductible expenses in terms of the tax benefit it generates, its impact is more positive because it does not generate a concurrent cash outflow. Amortization is also a non-cash charge, but the tax effects of amortization can vary depending upon the nature of the amortization. Some amortization, such as the amortization of the price paid for a patent or a trade mark, are tax deductible and reduce both accounting income and taxes. Thus, they provide tax benefits similar to depreciation. Other amortization, such as the amortization of the premium paid on an acquisition (called goodwill), reduces accounting income but not taxable income. This amortization does not provide a tax benefit.

Capital Expenditures and Depreciation

In project analysis, it is important that assumptions about capital expenditures, depreciation and working capital be consistent. For instance,

- If the project is assumed to have a very long life or an infinite life, the firm will have to make much larger capital maintenance expenditure. As a simple rule of thumb, when projects have infinite life, the capital maintenance expenditures should approach depreciation. This will, if nothing else, ensure that the book value of the investment does not decline. More importantly, it is necessary to preserve the earning power of the assets
- For projects with shorter lives, it is possible that capital expenditures occur up front, and that depreciation in subsequent years is much greater than capital expenditure. The book value of the investment will decline over time to the salvage value.

ROC, Cost of Capital, NPV and EVA

Economic value added is a value enhancement concept that has caught the attention of both firms interested in increasing their value and portfolio managers, looking for good investments. EVA is a measure of dollar surplus value created by a firm or project and is measured by doing the following:

Economic Value Added (EVA) = (Return on Capital-Cost of Capital) (Capital Invested) where the return on capital is measured using "adjusted" operating income, where the adjustments eliminate items that are unrelated to existing investments, and the capital investment is based upon the book value of capital, but is designed to measure the capital invested in existing assets. Firms which have positive EVA are firms which are creating surplus value, and firms with negative EVA are destroying value.

In the context of investment analysis, the present value of the EVA created by a project should be equal to the net present value of the project.

ROE, Cost of Equity and Equity EVA

While EVA is usually calculated using total capital, it can be easily modified to be an equity measure:

Equity EVA = (Return on Equity-Cost of Equity) (Equity Invested in Project or Firm)

Again, a firm which earns a positive equity EVA is creating value for its stockholders while a firm with a negative equity EVA is destroying value for its stockholders. Equity EVA may be the better way of thinking about value created for firms where capital is tough to measure (such as banks and insurance companies).

Equity Analysis versus Firm Analysis

An investment project can be analyzed in terms of all of the capital invested in the project (firm) or just from the perspective of the equity investors in the firm. If done consistently, cash flows to the firm discounted at the cost of capital or cash flows to equity discounted at the cost of equity, the two approaches should yield similar results if the following conditions hold:

a. The project is financed using the same mix of debt and equity as is used in the computation of the cost of capital.
b. The debt is assumed to have an interest rate equal to the pre-tax cost of debt

Currency Effects on Investment Analysis

One of the debates that analysts often engage in when doing investment analysis is whether the analysis should be done in one currency or another. Intuitively, an analysis of whether a project is a good or bad one should not depend upon what currency the analysis is done in. The important fact to keep in mind is that cash flows and the discount rate have to be estimated consistently. To convert the analysis from one currency to another would have required the following steps:

Step 1: Estimate the expected exchange rate for each period of the analysis.

While forward rates might be available for some currencies for a few periods, there are very few cases where forward rates will be available for the entire project life. To estimate the expected exchange rate, draw on the purchasing power parity theorem that argues that changes in exchange rates between two countries will reflect differences in inflation in those countries.

Step 2: Convert the expected cashflows from one currency to the other in future periods, using these exchange rates.

Step 3: Discount the expected cashflows at a discount rate, based upon the same currency.

Real versus Nominal Investment Analysis

Investment analyses can be done in terms of real or nominal cash flows. The discount rates have to be defined consistently-real for real cash flows and nominal for nominal cash flows. If done consistently, each analysis should yield the same net present value.

The choice between nominal and real cash flows therefore boils down to one of convenience. When inflation rates are low, it is better to do the analysis in nominal terms since taxes are based upon nominal income. When inflation rates are high and volatile, it is easier to do the analysis in real terms.

Given a choice, I would rather do the analysis in nominal terms, since taxes and financial statements are usually based upon nominal results.

Net Present Value, IRR or Modified IRR

For firms with no capital rationing constraints, net present value is clearly the choice that will maximize firm value the most.

For firms with significant capital rationing constraints that will continue into the future, the IRR is likely to be the best solution. For firms with significant capital rationing constraints that will ease over time, the modified IRR is the best solution.

Corporate Strategy and Project Quality

In the process of analyzing new investments in the preceding chapters, we have contended that good projects have a positive net present value and earn an internal rate of return greater than the hurdle rate. While these criteria are certainly valid from a measurement standpoint, they do not address the deeper questions about good projects including the economic conditions that make for a "good" project and why it is that some firms have a more ready supply of "good" projects than others.

Implicit in the definition of a good project--one that earns a return that is greater than that earned on investments of equivalent risk--is the existence of super-normal returns to the business considering the project. In a competitive market for real investments, the existence of these excess returns should act as a magnet, attracting competitors to take on similar investments. In the process, the excess returns should dissipate over time; how quickly they dissipate will depend on the ease with which competition can enter the market and provide close substitutes and on the magnitude of any differential advantages that the business with the good projects might possess. Take an extreme scenario, whereby the business with the good projects has no differential advantage in cost or product quality over its competitors, and new competitors can enter the market easily and at low cost to provide substitutes. In this case the super-normal returns on these projects should disappear very quickly.

An integral basis for the existence of a "good" project is the creation and maintenance of barriers to new or existing competitors taking on equivalent or similar projects. These barriers can take different forms, including

a. *Economies of Scale*: Some projects might earn high returns only if they are done on a "large" scale, thus restricting competition from smaller companies. In such cases, large companies in this line of business may be able to continue to earn super-normal returns on their projects because smaller competitors will not be able to replicate them.

b. *Cost Advantages*: A business might work at establishing a cost advantage over its competitors, either by being more efficient or by taking advantage of arrangements that its competitors cannot use. For example, in the late 1980s, Southwest Airlines was able to establish a cost advantage over its larger competitors, such as American and United Airlines by using non-union employees, the company exploited this cost advantage to earn much higher returns.

c. *Capital Requirements*: Entry into some businesses might require such large investments that it discourages competitors from entering, even though projects in those businesses may earn above-market returns. For example, assume that Boeing is faced with a large number of high-return projects in the aerospace business. While this scenario would normally attract competitors, the huge initial investment needed to enter this business would enable Boeing to continue to earn these high returns.

d. *Product Differentiation*: Some businesses continue to earn excess returns by differentiating their products from those of their competitors, leading to either higher profit margins or higher sales. This differentiation can be created in a number of ways-through effective advertising and promotion (Coca Cola), technical expertise (Sony), better service (Nordstrom) and responsiveness to customer needs.

e. *Access to Distribution Channels*: Those firms that have much better access to the distribution channels for their products than their competitors are better able to earn excess returns. In some cases, the restricted access to outsiders is due to tradition or loyalty to existing competitors. In other cases, the firm may actually own the distribution channel, and competitors may not be able to develop their own distribution channels because the costs are prohibitive.

f. *Legal and Government Barriers*: In some cases, a firm may be able to exploit investment opportunities without worrying about competition because of restrictions on competitors from product patents the firm may own to government restrictions on competitive entry. These arise, for instance, when companies are allowed to patent products or services, and gain the exclusive right to provide them over the patent life.

Management and Project Quality

In the preceding section we examined some of the factors that determine the attractiveness of the projects a firm will face. While some factors, such as government restrictions on entry, may largely be out of the control of incumbent management, there are other factors that can clearly be influenced by management may largely be out of the control of incumbent management, there are other factors that can clearly be influenced by management. Considering each of the factors discussed above, for instance, we would argue that a good management team can increase both the number of and the returns on available projects by

- taking projects that exploit any economies of scale that the firm may possess; in addition, management can look for ways it can create economies of scale in the firm's existing operations.
- establishing and nurturing cost advantages over its competitors; some cost advantages may arise from labour negotiations, while others may result from long-term strategic decisions made by the firm. For instance, by owning and developing SABRE, the airline reservation system, American Airlines has been able to gain a cost advantage over its competitors.
- taking actions that increase the initial cost for new entrants into the business; one of the primary reasons Microsoft's was able to dominate the computer software market in the early 1990s was its ability to increase the investment needed to develop and market software programs.
- increasing brand name recognition and value through advertising and by delivering superior products to customers; a good example is the success that Snapple

experienced in the early 1990s in promoting and selling its iced tea beverages.

- nurturing markets in which the company's differential advantage is greatest, in terms of either cost of delivery or brand name value. In some cases, this will involve expanding into foreign markets, as both Levi Strauss and McDonalds did in the 1980s in order to exploit their higher brand name recognition in those markets. In other cases, this may require concentrating on segments of an existing market as The Gap did, when it opened its Banana Republic division, which sells upscale outdoor clothing.
- improving the firm's reputation for customer service and product delivery; this will enable the firm to increase both profits and returns. One of the primary factors behind Chrysler's financial recovery in the 1980s was the company's ability to establish a reputation for producing quality cars and minivans.
- developing distribution channels that are unique and cannot be easily accessed by competitors. Avon, for instance, employed large sales force to go door-to-door to reach consumers who could not be reached by other distribution channels.
- getting patents on products or technologies that keep out the competition and earn high returns; doing so may require large investments in research and development over time. It can be argued that Intel's success in the market for semiconductors can be traced to the strength of its research and development efforts and the patents it consequently obtained on advanced chips, such as the Pentium.

While the quality of management is typically related to the quality of projects a firm possesses, a good management team does not guarantee the existence of good projects. In fact, there is a rather large element of chance involved in the process; even the best laid plans of the management team to create project opportunities may come to naught if circumstances conspire against them-a recession may upend a retailer, or an oil price shock may cause an airline to lose money.

Working Capital Management

Defining Working Capital

The term working capital refers to the amount of capital which is readily available to an organisation. That is, working capital is the difference between resources in cash or readily convertible into cash (Current Assets) and organisational commitments for which cash will soon be required (Current Liabilities).

Current Assets are resources which are in cash or will soon be converted into cash in "the ordinary course of business".

Current Liabilities are commitments which will soon require cash settlement in "the ordinary course of business".

Thus:

WORKING CAPITAL = CURRENT ASSETS-CURRENT LIABILITIES

In a department's Statement of Financial Position, these components of working capital are reported under the following headings:

Current Assets

- Liquid Assets (cash and bank deposits)
- Inventory
- Debtors and Receivables

Current Liabilities

- Bank Overdraft
- Creditors and Payables
- Other Short Term Liabilities

The Importance of Good Working Capital Management

Working capital constitutes part of the Crown's investment in a department. Associated with this is an opportunity cost to the Crown. (Money invested in one area may "cost" opportunities for investment in other areas.) If a department is operating with more working capital than is necessary, this over-investment represents an unnecessary cost to the Crown. From a department's point of view, excess working capital means operating inefficiencies. In addition, unnecessary working capital increases the amount of the capital charge which departments are required to meet from 1 July 1991.

Approaches to Working Capital Management

The objective of working capital management is to maintain the optimum balance of each of the working capital components. This includes making sure that funds are held as cash in bank deposits for as long as and in the largest amounts possible, thereby maximising the interest earned. However, such cash may more appropriately be "invested" in other assets or in reducing other liabilities.

Working capital management takes place on two levels:

- Ratio analysis can be used to monitor overall trends in working capital and to identify areas requiring closer management.
- The individual components of working capital can be effectively managed by using various techniques and strategies.

When considering these techniques and strategies, departments need to recognise that each department has a unique mix of working capital components. The emphasis that needs to be placed on each component varies according to department. For example, some departments have significant inventory levels; others have little if any inventory. Furthermore, working capital management is not an end in itself. It is an integral part of the department's overall management. The needs of efficient working capital management must be considered in relation to other aspects of the department's financial and non-financial performance.

Financial Ratio Analysis

Financial ratio analysis calculates and compares various ratios of amounts and balances taken from the financial statements.

The main purposes of working capital ratio analysis are:

- to indicate working capital management performance; and
- to assist in identifying areas requiring closer management.

Three key points need to be taken into account when analyzing financial ratios:

- The results are based on highly summarised information. Consequently, situations which require control might not be apparent, or situations which do not warrant significant effort might be unnecessarily highlighted;
- Different departments face very different situations. Comparisons between them, or with global "ideal" ratio values, can be misleading;
- Ratio analysis is somewhat one-sided; favourable results mean little, whereas unfavourable results are usually significant.

However, financial ratio analysis is valuable because it raises questions and indicates directions for more detailed investigation.

The following ratios are of interest to those managing working capital:

- working capital ratio;
- liquid interval measure;
- stock turnover;
- debtors ratio;
- creditors ratio.

Working Capital Ratio

Current Assets divided by Current Liabilities

The working capital ratio (or current ratio) attempts to measure the level of liquidity, that is, the level of safety provided by the excess of current assets over current liabilities.

The "quick ratio" a derivative, excludes inventories from the current assets, considering only those assets most swiftly realisable.

There are also other possible refinements. There is no particular benchmark value or range that can be recommended as suitable for all government departments. However, if a department tracks its own working capital ratio over a period of time, the trends-the way in which the liquidity is changing-will become apparent.

Liquid Interval Measure

Liquid Assets divided by Average Operating Expenses

This is another measure of liquidity. It looks at the number of days that liquid assets (for example, inventory) could service daily operating expenses (including salaries).

Stock Turnover

Cost of Sales divided by Average Stock Level

This ratio applies only to finished goods. It indicates the speed with which inventory is sold-or, to look at it from the other angle, how long inventory items remain on the shelves. It can be used for the inventory balance as a whole, for classes of inventory, or for individual inventory items. The figure produced by the stock turnover ratio is not important in itself, but the trend over time is a good indicator of the validity of changes in inventory policies.

In general, a higher turnover ratio indicates that a lower level of investment is required to serve the department.

Most departments do not hold significant inventories of finished goods, so this ratio will have only limited relevance.

Debtor Ratio

There is a close relationship between debtors and credit sales to third parties (that is, sales other than to the Crown). If sales increase, debtors will increase, and conversely, if sales decrease debtors will decrease. The best way to explain this relationship is to express it as the number of days that credit sales are carried on the books:

Credit Sales per Period x Days per Period

Average Debtors: Where trading terms are 30 days net cash, and customers buy from day-to-day during the 30 day period and pay 30 days after a statement is rendered, a collection period of 45 days (the average between 30 and 60 days) would be satisfactory.

If the average collection period extends beyond 60 days, debtors are holding cash that should have flowed into the department. This means that the department is unable to satisfy pressing liabilities or to invest that cash.

The debtor ratio does not solve the collection problem, but it acts as an indicator that an adverse trend is developing. Remedial action can then be instigated.

Creditor Ratio

This ratio is much the same as the debtor ratio. It expresses the relationship between credit purchases and the liability to creditors. It can be stated as the number of days that credit purchases are carried on the books.

Credit Purchases per Period × Days per Period

Average Creditors: Note that non-credit purchases (such as salaries) and non-cash expenses (such as depreciation) need to be excluded from "credit purchases" and any provisions need to be excluded from "creditors".

There is no need to pay creditors before payment is due. The department's objective should be to make effective use of this source of free credit, while maintaining a good relationship with creditors.

As with debtors, if a department has been granted credit terms of 30 days net cash, credit purchases should not be carried on the books for more than an average of 45 days. If payment is withheld for 60 days or more it is likely that creditors will become impatient and impose stricter and less convenient trading terms-for example, "cash on delivery".

The Public Finance Act 1989 (section 49) places a legal constraint on the amount of credit allowed to a department. It restricts to a maximum of 90 days the purchase of goods and services through the use of a credit card or suppliers' credit.

Specific Strategies

Inventories

Inventories are lists of stocks-raw materials, work in progress or finished goods-waiting to be consumed in production or to be sold.

The total balance of inventory is the sum of the value of each individual stock line. Stock records are needed:

- to provide an account of activity within each stock line;
- as evidence to support the balances used in financial reports.

A department also needs a system of internal controls to efficiently manage stocks and to ensure that stock records provide reliable information.

Departmental financial reports show only the total inventory balance. Analysts from outside the department can examine this balance by using ratio analysis or other techniques. However, this gives only a limited assessment of inventory management and is not adequate for internal management. Good financial management necessitates the careful analysis of individual inventory lines.

Inventory management is an important aspect of working capital management because inventories themselves do not earn any revenue. Holding either too little or too much inventory incurs costs.

Costs of carrying too much inventory are:

- opportunity cost of foregone interest;
- warehousing costs;
- damage and pilferage;
- obsolescence;
- insurance.

Costs of carrying too little inventory are:

- stockout costs:
  - * lost sales;

   * delayed service.

- ordering costs:

   * freight;
   * order administration;
   * loss of quantity discounts.

Carrying costs can be minimised by making frequent small orders but this increases ordering costs and the risk of stock-outs. Risk of stock-outs can be reduced by carrying "safety stocks" (at a cost) and re-ordering ahead of time.

The best ordering strategy requires balancing the various cost factors to ensure the department incurs minimum inventory costs. The optimum inventory position is known as the Economic Reorder Quantity (ERQ). There are a number of mathematical models (of varying complexity) for calculating ERQ. (Any standard accounting text will provide examples of these).

Analytical review of inventories can help to identify areas where inventory management can be improved. Slow moving items, continual stockouts, obsolescence, stock reconciliation problems and excess spoilage are signals that stock lines need closer analysis and control.

However, it is important to keep an overall perspective. It is not cost-effective to closely manage a large number of low value inventory lines, nor is it necessary. A usual feature of inventories is that a small number of high value lines account for a large proportion of inventory value.

The "80/20" rule (PARETO) predicts that 80% of the total value of inventory is represented by only 20% of the number of inventory items. Those high value lines need reasonably close management. The remaining 80% of inventory lines can be managed using "broad-brush" strategies.

The overall management philosophy of an organisation can affect the way in which inventory is managed.

For example, "Just In Time" (JIT) production management organises production so that finished goods are not produced until the customer needs them (minimising finished goods carrying costs), and raw materials are not accepted from suppliers until they are needed. (Large organisations have the power to insist that suppliers hold stocks of raw materials and thereby pass the carrying cost back to the supplier).

Thus, JIT inventory strategies reduce bottlenecks and stock holding costs.

In summary:

- There is a trade-off to be made between carrying costs, ordering costs, and stockout costs. This is represented in the Economic Reorder Quantity (ERQ) model.
- Inventories should be managed on a line-by-line basis using the 80/20 rule.
- Analytical review can help to focus attention on critical areas.
- Inventory management is part of the overall management strategy.

Debtors

Debtors (Accounts Receivable) are customers who have not yet made payment for goods or services which the department has provided. The objective of debtor management is to minimise the time-lapse between completion of sales and receipt of payment. The costs of having debtors are:

- opportunity costs (cash is not available for other purposes);
- bad debts.

Debtor management includes both pre-sale and debt collection strategies.

Pre-sale strategies include:

- offering cash discounts for early payment and/or imposing penalties for late payment;
- agreeing payment terms in advance;
- requiring cash before delivery;
- setting credit limits;

- setting criteria for obtaining credit;
- billing as early as possible;
- requiring deposits and/or progress payments.

Post-sale strategies include:

- Placing the responsibility for collecting the debt upon the center that made the sale;
- Identifying long overdue balances and doubtful debts by regular analytical reviews;
- Having an established procedure for late collections, such as
    * a reminder;
    * a letter;
    * cancellation of further credit;
    * telephone calls;
    * use of a collection agency;
    * legal action.

Creditors

Creditors (Accounts Payable) are suppliers whose invoices for goods or services have been processed but who have not yet been paid. Organisations often regard the amount owing to creditors as a source of free credit. However, creditor administration systems are expensive and time-consuming to run. The overriding concern in this area should be to minimise costs with simple procedures.

While it is unnecessary to pay accounts before they fall due, it is usually not worthwhile to delay all payments until the latest possible date., Regular weekly or fortnightly payment of all due accounts is the simplest technique for creditor management.

Electronic payments (direct credits) are cheaper than cheque payments, considering that transaction fees and overheads more than balance the advantage of delayed presentation. Some suppliers are reluctant to receive payments by this method, but in view of the substantial cost advantage (and the advantages to the suppliers themselves) departments may wish to encourage suppliers to accept this option. However, electronic payments are likely to be used in conjunction with, rather than as a replacement for, cheque payments.

Cash and Bank

Good cash management can have a major impact on overall working capital management.

The key elements of cash management are:

- cash forecasting;
- balance management;
- administration;
- internal control.

Cash Forecasting: Good cash management requires regular forecasts. In order for these to be materially accurate, they must be based on information provided by those managers responsible for the amounts and timing of expenditure. Capital expenditure and operating expenditure must be taken into account. It is also necessary to collect information about impending cash transactions from other financial systems, such as creditors and payroll.

Balance Management: Those responsible for balance management must make decisions about how much cash should at any time be on call in the Departmental Bank Account and how much should be on term deposit at the various terms available.

There are various types of mathematical model that can be used. One type is analogous to the ERQ inventory model. Linear programming models have been developed for cash management, subject to certain constraints. There are also more sophisticated techniques.

Administration: Cash receipts should be processed and banked as quickly as possible because:

- They cannot earn interest or reduce overdraft until they are banked;
- Information about the existence and amounts of cash receipts is usually not available until they are processed.

Where possible, cash floats (mainly petty cash and advances) should be avoided. If, on review, the only reason that can be put forward for their existence is that "we've always had them", they should be discontinued. There may be situations where they are useful, however. For example, it may be desirable for peripheral parts of departments to meet urgent local needs from cash floats rather than local bank accounts.

Internal Control: Cash and cash management is part of a department's overall internal control system. The main internal cash control is invariably the bank reconciliation. This provides assurance that the cash balances recorded in the accounting systems are consistent with the actual bank balances. It requires regular clearing of reconciling items.

Other Components

Working capital, defined as the difference between current assets and current liabilities, may also include the following factors:

- prepayments to creditors;
- current portions of long-term liabilities;
- revenue received before it has been earned;
- provisions.

However, decisions on working capital management usually exclude these factors, so they have not been included in this booklet.

Summary

Good management of working capital is part of good financial management. Effective use of working capital will contribute to the operational efficiency of a department; optimum use will help to generate maximum returns.

Ratio analysis can be used to identify working capital areas which require closer management. Various techniques and strategies are available for managing specific working capital items.

Debtors, creditors, cash and in some cases inventories are the areas most likely to be relevant to departments.

4

The Measurement of Hospitality

Managing Change: Performance Measurement for Destination

Management Organizations

In recent years, tourist destinations managers have been criticized because of their inability to reinvent themselves in face of the radical changes in the external environment. The tourism industry is in a state of unprecedented change. Indeed, the first few years of the new millennium have brought extraordinary change and transformation. War, terrorism, political upheaval, the spread of infectious diseases, airline restructuring and the advancement and use of technology are just a few of the events that are having a profound impact on destinations' performance around the world.

It appears, however, that many DMO executives are unable to manage change and find it increasingly difficult to determine the impact these events are likely to have on the destination and on destination management organizations. The pressure exerted by competition is compelling international, national, state, and local governments to re-evaluate the existing tourism resources and to capitalize on them in order to attract more visitors (Fayos-Sola, 1996).

As King (2002) points out, "nothing short of a reinvention of destination marketing organizations (DMOs) will ensure they are able to keep abreast of and capitalize upon the revolution taking place". In a highly competitive tourism market, it is increasingly important to understand the role each destination plays in relation to other competitive destinations.

The strategic responses to these developments are essentially decisions on whether to proactively shape or reactively adapt to the crisis. Deciding on which strategic orientation to choose in response to current developments is essentially a decision on whether to shape or adapt to the crisis.

Mapping your Strategy and Measures

Organizational effectiveness depends on the ability of the organization to adapt to its environment, which is in turn influenced primarily by the strategic management of the organization. An effective monitoring of external forces should help identify not only emerging opportunities and threats, but also the organization's strengths and weaknesses for meeting these opportunities and threats. Organizations are shaped by their performance measure. Performance measures play a critical role in formulating corporate strategies, evaluating accomplishments, and compensating organizational members. Performance measures and outcomes are predetermined methods for assessing whether the aforementioned goals and objectives are achieved.

Lebas and Euske (2002) provide a good definition of performance as "doing today what will lead to measured value outcomes tomorrow." Business Performance Measurement (BPM) then is concerned with measuring this performance relative to some benchmark, be it a competitor's performance or a preset target. Business performance, which reflects the perspective of strategic management, is a subset of the overall concept of organizational effectiveness.

A specific measure can be compared to itself over time, compared with a preset target or evaluated along with other measures. Since a measure is used for the purpose of comparison, it need not represent an absolute value. Following Simmons (2000), measures can be objective or subjective. Objective measures can be independently measured and verified. Subjective ones cannot. Measures are also typically classified as financial or non-financial.

Financial measures are typically derived from or directly related to the chart of accounts and found in a company's profit and loss statement or balance sheet, such as inventory levels or cash on hand. Non-financial measures are measures not found in the chart of accounts, such as customer satisfaction scores or product quality measures. Measures are also leading or lagging. Lagging measures give feedback on past performance, such as last month's profit, and typically do not provide insight into future performance. Leading indicators, in contrast, are designed to measure future performance, and more often than not, future financial performance.

It is important to note that performance measurement itself has no consequence: simply knowing that there is scope for improvement in an organization because you have measured some aspect of its performance will not, in itself, lead to any improvement. So in order to get some improvement as a result of performance measurement, the organization needs to do something in the light of this information. The issues associated with 'doing something in the light of performance measurement data' are covered by the more general topic of *performance* management.

Perspectives of Performance Measurement

The field of performance measurement has evolved rapidly in the last few years with the development of new measurement approaches, frameworks and methodologies, such as the economic value added, shareholder value added, activity based costing, cost of quality, competitive benchmarking and balanced scorecard. Each framework purports to be unique and appears to claim comprehensiveness, yet each offers a different perspective on performance.

Developed by the Stern Stewart Corporation as an overall measure of financial performance, economic value added (EVA) is both a specific performance measure and the basis for a larger performance measurement framework (Otley, 1999). According to its creators, EVA is a financial performance metric that is most directly linked to the creation of shareholder value, over time. EVA is net operating profit less an appropriate charge for the opportunity cost of all capital invested in an enterprise. However, using EVA alone can cause managers to invest in less risky, cost-reducing activities rather than in growth activities and as a pure financial model, EVA cannot serve as a vehicle for articulating a strategy. Shareholder value frameworks incorporate the cost of capital into the equation, but ignore everything (and everyone) else.

Activity-based costing (ABC) was developed to provide better insight into how overhead costs should be allocated to individual products or customers. ABC links expenses related to the resources supplied to the organization with the activities performed within the organization. Expenses flow from resources to activities and then to products, services and customers. Both activity based costing and cost of quality, on the other hand, focus on the identification and control of cost drivers (nonvalue-adding activities and failures/nonconformances respectively), which are themselves often embedded in the business processes. But this highly process focused view ignores any other perspectives on performance – such as the opinion of shareholders, customers and employees. Conversely, benchmarking tends to involve taking a largely external perspective, often comparing performance with that of competitors or other 'best practitioners' of business processes.

Kaplan and David P. Norton in 1992, balanced scorecards have found widespread adoption in varied industries. Initially focused on finding a way to report on leading indicators of a business's health rather than traditional accounting measures which are lagging indicators, the balanced scored was refocused to measure the firm's strategy. Instead of measuring anything, firms should measure those things that directly relate to the firm's strategy. The balanced scorecard is broken down into four sections, called perspectives: The financial perspective relates to the strategy for growth, profitability and risk from the shareholder's perspective. The customer perspective relates to the strategy for creating value and differentiation from the perspective of the customer.

The internal business perspective relates to the strategic priorities for various business processes that create customer and shareholder satisfaction. The learning and growth perspective relates to the priorities to create a climate that supports organizational change, innovation and growth. The balanced scorecard, with its four perspectives, focuses on financials (shareholders), customers, internal processes, plus innovation and learning. In doing so it downplays the importance of other stakeholders, such as suppliers and employees. By combining these different perspectives, the balanced scorecard helps managers understand the interrelationships and tradeoffs between alternative performance dimensions and leads to improved decision making and problem solving. The characteristic feature of *'balance'* is supposed to be guaranteed by considering short-long term/financial and non-financial/lagging and leading indicators, concerning four perspectives.

One might reasonably ask, how can multiple, and seemingly inconsistent, business performance frameworks and measurement methodologies exist? They can exist because they all add value. They all provide unique perspectives on performance. They all furnish managers with a different set of lenses through which they can assess the performance of their organizations. Firms adapt these frameworks for a variety of reasons, but chiefly to improve control over the firm in ways that traditional accounting systems have not allowed. If the organization wishes to implement a major change in its strategy, a BSC scheme may be embarked upon first and then the missing elements can be captured with the help of other frameworks. Using this approach, companies get insights into profitable and profitless activities based on a customer or a product viewpoint.

However, organizations in some industries have also modified the balanced scorecard in order to fit their business models.

Benefits of Performance Measurement

Measurement plays a crucial role in translating business strategy into results (Lingle & Schiemann, 1996). Performance measures or indicators are measurable characteristics of products, services, processes, and operations the company uses to track and improve performance. The measures or indicators should be selected to best represent the factors that lead to improved customer, operational, and financial performance. A comprehensive set of measures or indicators tied to customer and/or company performance requirements represents a clear basis for aligning all activities with the company's goals. Through the analysis of data from the tracking processes, the measures or indicators themselves may be evaluated and changed to better support such goals. Numerous researchers have discussed the link between strategy, measurement and success. Those that measure gain agreement on the strategy, clarity of communication, focus and alignment and organizational culture advantages. Strategy and performance measurements need to be intertwined, and as such are likely to be unique for each organization. Organizations should measure how parts of their value chain actually fit together for an overarching advantage instead of relying on process-byprocess metrics (Porter, 2002).

Measuring results facilitates early identification and correction of problems at the source, before they require correcting from the outside. A key attribute for the BSC and other BPM frameworks is the support for identifying and communicating causal linkages between components of the business that fulfill the strategy. Identifying the causal linkages may be a bottleneck. If data show a drop in success, a quick diagnosis can identify the reasons and suggest immediate remedies. At the most basic level, metrics tell us what is working and what is not. DMOs can provide better service to its stakeholders while avoiding the necessity of having remedies imposed from the outside.

Performance Measurement Systems

The level of performance a business attains is a function of the efficiency and effectiveness of the actions it undertakes. This not only identifies two fundamental dimensions of performance, but also highlights the fact that there can be internal as well as external reasons for pursuing specific courses of action (Slack, 1991).The mechanics of performance measurement are complex and the development and deployment of the process painful. Typically many measures will be reported and tracked before a key set will emerge. Many choices will be driven by industry best practices measures so that a competitive benchmarking program can be established. Many will be reported in order to establish a baseline well before a target improvement value is established. A balance between breath, completeness and complexity and competitive comparison must be developed. Business Performance Measurement/Management can be done at two distinct levels: strategic and operational. The balanced scorecard is an example of a strategic BPM. Operational BPM help managers with specific operational process control issues that may or may not be directly related to the strategy however are crucial to develop the organizations BSC and hence contribute to the overall success of the organization. The key to successful performance measurement is to identify and collect meaningful performance measures that can or actually will be used.

Once a firm becomes large enough that a single manager cannot sense the firm's current state and cannot control its behavior alone, the firm must use performance measurement and control systems to replace the eyes and ears of the beleaguered manager. Over the past few decades, firms have used information technology to provide this "sense and control" capability. Performance measurement system is a widely applied management tool which can be used to assess an organization's progress towards achieving its predefined goals, which include the efficiency with which resources are transformed into goods and services, the quality of these goods and services, the results of a program activity compared to its intended purpose and the effectiveness of operations in terms of their specific contributions to the organization's objectives. The system tools can leverage the latest advancements in data and application integration approaches, web-based charting and reporting, statistical analysis, artificial intelligence, machine learning and expert system technology.

Implementing a performance measurement system can significantly enhance an organization's capacity to successfully leverage information and data. More importantly, this can help an organization foster a culture that is largely focused on strategy, learning, and continuous improvement through monitoring and measuring its own performance. It is crucial that performance measures will provide an organization with tools to examine and formulate their strategies. This entails measures that are indicative of procedures, processes, and strategies of investing in and building long-term resources, facilities, and infrastructure as needed to adapt to the fast pace of today's changing environments.

At the lowest level of analysis lies measurement of human performance and the overall organizational performance is the ultimate level of evaluation. In between the overall organization effectiveness and the individual lie other layers, such as the functional or service group, workgroup or team and the business activity. Performance Measurement systems are often designed to be a vehicle for strategic dialog within the firms. System tools enable individuals to record and discover discrepancies between stated goals and actual performance creating a favourable learning environment which in turn facilitates organizational change. Technology allows storing and retrieving relevant actual performance information for future comparison and decision making.

Performance Measurement Systems can help provide this firmwide coherency and enable decision makers to bundle measures based on their cognitive understanding and knowledge of the organizational environment. These systems facilitate coherence of performance metrics and scorecards, scattered horizontally and vertically across an organization, so that the conversations between people about the strategy is consistent and all the different measurement units contribute to the performance of the organization as a whole.

Future of Performance Measurement in Tourism

Traditionally, the tourism industry has used visitor satisfaction studies, conversion studies, and economic impact models as indicators to evaluate the performance of a destination. However, these measures do not provide a clear understanding of the impacts on the destination performance generated by the efforts of the DMO. As a result, CVBs would sometimes find themselves limited in their ability to systematically and credibly articulate their contribution to the destination. To address this problem *A Handbook for CVBs* is published by the Destination Marketing Association

International formerly, International Association of Convention and Visitor Bureaus (IACVB). The association represents nearly 600 destination management organizations in over 30 countries. The Performance Measurement Team (PMT) recently created by the Destination Marketing Association International has recommended bureaus use a standard business return-on-investment formula to quantify the financial impact on its local community for convention and leisure travel. By using the standard corporate business valuation model, PMT has developed a definitive Return on Investment (ROI) formula for bureaus to apply.

IACVB claims that with the adoption of these industry standards, a CVB will have recognized benchmarks to utilize for assessing internal performance, as well as a means to accurately compare performance with other CVBs. It is IACVB's intent that the handbook on performance reporting (IACVB, 2005) will aid the decision making process for resource allocation, sales and marketing campaign development, as well as staff training and development. IACVB continues to build on its long-standing commitment to provide strategic and operational guidance to convention and visitor bureaus (CVBs). Through the development of standards, best practices and systematic approaches to organizational functions, CVBs are able to employ comparative analytical tools in identifying organizational strengths, weaknesses, and opportunities.

In addition to internally reviewing their operations, CVBs are often required, due to their unique funding sources, to undergo external performance reviews by various stakeholders within their local communities. At times, these external audits/reviews may be done by firms lacking CVB knowledge and experience. As a result, CVBs' achievements were underreported and misunderstood, a circumstance potentially damaging to the relationship between the CVB and its stakeholders. Most bureaus are classified as independent, not-for profit organizations, but some are part of city or county governments while others have special legal authority. Further, because bureaus vary in terms of their structure, scope, size, geographic location and type of management the standard measures might sometimes be misleading if these differences are not taken into consideration.

The IACVB's standard measures fail to recognize that the external environment, often referred to as the organizational environment, are different for all CVBs. The external environment consist of all elements outside the boundary of the organization and includes elements of competition, resources, technology, economic conditions and other elements that may in some way be related to the performance of the organization. As all DMOs belong to the same tourism industry they are likely to select some measures that are similar (mainly process measures), but they also need to identify a number of measures that are unique to each one of them and are a reflection of differences in their long-term goals and in the specific issues they face, despite being in the same industry.

Smart-Perform for Destination Management Organizations

Incremental strategic change may be successful in fairly stable environments. However, in order to survive in the dynamic environment DMOs need to establish relationships with all important partners and prove that they know what they are doing. Understanding the link between environmental characteristics and performance has several important implications for the way in which DMOs plan for the future. In order to facilitate this, the National Laboratory of Tourism & eCommerce at School of Tourism and Hospitality Management, Temple University is developing a performance

measurement system, SMART-PERFORM, specially catering to the DMOs. This system is designed to address the increasing information needs by integrating historical, present (near real time) and future (forecasts) data which is critical for the design and implementation of a DMOs marketing/communication programs or campaigns. Based upon the information, the system will help bureaus establish a series of performance criteria with which to evaluate their marketing efforts and resource based/ capacity building aspects of the organization. More specifically, the system will benefit the bureau in terms of:

- Systematic performance appraisals;
- Useful, timely, and credible market information;
- Improved visitor satisfaction;
- Fostering accountability and responsibility;
- Improved managerial decision making; and,
- More meaningful and easy-to-understand information that can be presented to stakeholders.

In the process of adopting and implementing the bureau will go through a process to outline their measures and set up baseline measures (the first measure taken) of a current processes, work output or organizational outcome results which could then be used for benchmarking against other like programs or CVBs. As a performance measurement system, Smart-perform involves the collection, synthesis, delivery, and display of information related to the measurement of productivity output and accomplishment, as well as in-process parameters that affect productivity. If the results differ from goals and objectives, the bureau members can analyse the gaps in performance and make adjustments. A model for measuring the bureau's performance will help all members-customers, suppliers, employees, and community understand and evaluate their contributions and expectations.

Performance measurement is an evolving, iterative challenge. The Perform system developed especially for each participating DMO will help the bureau executives to make decisions regarding critical organizational issue such as depth/quality of strategic planning, indicators of partnerships and alliances, anticipating and preparing for changes in the environment, and investments in new markets and technologies. This will be an efficient and effective management tool which will empower managers to both monitor past performance and stimulate future action.

The Development and Planning

The delivery of quality products and services, within international tourism and hospitality, reflects an increasing focus on intangibles and the role of what can be styled the "human factor". Companies struggle to create clear distinction and consumer recognition of added value on the basis of physical product differentiation (Balmer and Baum, 1993) except within a relatively limited band of the market. Airline brand relaunches (new first-and business-class products) and the executive floor products, within the hotel sector, represent a small proportion of the global market and trends in this direction are counter-balanced by the growing strength of budget or economy products (hotels and no-frills airlines) in Europe and North America, catering for both the leisure and business customer.

There is considerable evidence to support the notion that there has been a merging of the tourism experience, in physical product terms, across the range of designated quality levels. The introduction of "Business First" products by airlines offers consumers what is claimed to be a first-class environment for business-class price, while budget to mid-range hotel rooms offer a range of facilities which are not significantly different from some products in the four-star range. This trend is one which has, in part, created the need to focus on service delivery as an alternative differentiator in the marketplace. The Marriott empowerment series of advertisements is a good example of recognition of this focus by a major hospitality corporation.

A "people" focus, within tourism and hospitality, is by no means new and successful organizations such as Disney, British Airways, Singapore Airlines, Marriott and Ritz Carlton have developed strong reputations for their recognition of the role which their staff play in meeting customer expectations within their sector. As a consequence, this is an area which has been studied and analysed in considerable depth, and the literature represents a significant collection of empirical research, good practice case-studies and rather polemical "how to wow the customer" pieces. The focus of such work is at the level of the firm and much of it builds on the work of major corporations such as those identified above. Best practice, in the area, appears to recognize that quality service delivery is not the outcome of an isolated service enhancement training programme, but has to do with change in organizational culture from top down and is a complex process which impacts on all areas of the organization and its systems (Mahesh, 1994). It is also a process which is rather more commonly taken aboard within the context of larger organizations. Small to medium-sized enterprises (SMEs), which have the advantage of simple internal communication systems, face other challenges reflective of their resource structures, expertise and nature of their workforce.

There is little doubt that consumer experience of "human value added" through service is varied within and between the hospitality sectors of most countries. In part, this is a reflection of the eclectic nature of customer expectations which may demand very different things from the same service delivery situation. It is also a factor of the number of human interactions (moments of truth) which most customers experience within any one hospitality purchase-these may or may not be within the one organization and thus the ability to "control" the customer's experience may not lie within the organization, which suffers through lost business. In many respects, a customer's assessment of hospitality will be based on the total destination experience.

This article develops the argument that human resource management is more than a strategic and operational concern for companies competing within the hospitality marketplace. It considers human resource management as a strategic dimension within the wider enhancement of quality and market positioning of tourism at the level of organizations, specific destinations, regions within countries or whole nations.

The main thesis advanced is that the tourism and hospitality industry, from the perspective of all its stakeholders (public sector, private sector, visitors and host community), benefits from the close integration of human resource, labour market and education policies, with those policies relating to, and impacting on, the tourism and hospitality sector. This thesis is developed by reporting key findings from two research projects which address aspects of the relationship between these two areas of policy. The first is concerned with the identification of key future policy priorities for human resource development in tourism and hospitality, while the second addresses the structures and policy formulation environment necessary for creation of effective linkages between tourism and hospitality, on the one hand, and education, training and development on the other.

Human Resource Policy Issues in Tourism and Hospitality

The tourism and hospitality sector, in all locations, has a close relationship with the labour market environment from which it draws its skills and consequently depends on its workforce for the delivery of service and product standards to meet existing and anticipated demand from its visitor marketplace. This relationship is, on the one hand, one of dependency in that the make-up of the local workforce (or that which can be introduced into the local environment) has a direct influence on the standards and character of the tourist offering which can be prepared and presented to visitors-if local art and craft skills are not developed within the education system or at community level, it will not be possible to offer this dimension to visitors. On the other hand, tourism and hospitality, for many communities, provides a major and growing sector of the economy and, with it, employment opportunities which other traditional and declining sectors of the economy may not provide.

This is true in an industrial, urban context where cities such as Glasgow (now the second most visited urban centre in the UK) have developed tourism in the wake of the decline of its traditional heavy industrial sector. It is an equally valid scenario in locations where the exploitation of natural resources no longer provides the same level of employment opportunity as it did in the past-the decline of the North Atlantic fishery has seen island locations, such as the Faroes, Iceland, Greenland and Newfoundland, focus on tourism as part of wider economic diversification strategies. As one of the studies reported in this article illustrates, the two-way relationship between tourism and hospitality, and human resource development and management is not always recognized in a holistic and policy-focused manner by public or private sector concerns.

Writing in 1993, Baum identified a number of what were described as "universal themes": issues which literature and practical experience identified as the major human resource concerns faced by tourism and hospitality at both a practical, operational level and in the context of wider strategic and policy-oriented discussion. These were:

Demography and the shrinking employment pool resulting in labour and specific skills shortages. This is primarily a developed country phenomenon found in Western Europe, North America and "tiger economy" countries of the Far East. However, labour shortage is also a concern elsewhere when it is recognized that the specific skills which tourism demands (technical, cultural, communications) may be in short supply within many, less developed destination areas. Demographic and other forms of structural change within the labour market demand responses which take tourism recruitment beyond its traditional youth pool into consideration of mature worker alternatives (those returning to work; seeking a career change; retirees) and this, in turn, has major implications for relative remuneration, working conditions, employment security and related issues.

For many subsectors in tourism and hospitality, and in most developed countries, the negative employment image of the sector is a major issue and barrier to the recruitment and retention of quality and well educated employees (Choy, 1995). Wood (1995) argues that "both industry employees and wider society view hotel and catering labour as relatively low status, mainly because of the personal service nature of the work involved". This poor image is the result of a cocktail of historic and contemporary factors-the origin of hospitality work within domestic service and its consequent associations with servility; links, in some countries, between hospitality employment and colonial legacy; widespread use of expatriate labour in many developing countries, creating the perception that the sector is one offering only limited opportunity for promotion and progression; widespread exposure to work in the sector as a first working experience, resulting in generalized assessment based on limited exposure; and the reality of antisocial working conditions and casualized remuneration.

In some respects, the negatively-held perceptions are not wholly justified by the reality of work for major airlines, international hotel groups, theme parks or within heritage organizations. In other regards, the perceptions are a mirror of the reality of work within an industrial sector dominated by small and medium-sized enterprises (SMEs) and the impact of irregular demand.

The effect of these perceptions is to impose a barrier to employment and employment choice among school and college leavers, parents and career guidance teachers which has been very difficult to counter. However, the situation, in some developing countries, is rather different in that international tourism offers a high status and secure employment environment when compared to alternatives in both the primary and manufacturing sectors.

In some contexts, cultural and traditional perceptions may also militate against the recruitment of the best able and qualified recruits into the tourism and hospitality sector. Religious barriers, for example, may exclude some groups from participation, notably women. As already indicated, the rewards and benefits structure of the tourism and hospitality industries can act as a barrier to the recruitment and retention of quality employees. This is a concern of particular focus within hospitality but perceptions regarding working conditions, hours and pay extend more generally across the tourism-related service sector.

There is a clear and unavoidable reality, within tourism and hospitality, that the demand cycle is antisocial and falls out with "normal" nine-to-five working parameters. Aircraft fly at night, hotel guests expect services at weekends and theme parks reach peak demand during public holidays. In terms of remuneration, the sector faces challenges in common with other labour-intensive service areas and in many countries has seen pressures for increased productivity alongside deskilling in many areas of work. At a policy level, the sector is influenced greatly by legislative intervention, for example European initiatives with respect to minimum wage levels, duration of the working week and unsociable working times.

Notwithstanding national and sub-sectoral diversity within tourism and hospitality, a combination of reality and perceptions gives an overall negative gloss to the image of many areas of the industry. As we have already suggested, this acts as a major barrier to the recruitment of quality personnel into work in the area. Many entrants to work in the sector do so with expectations of impermanence-this reflects reality in terms of the demand cycle (seasonality and fluctuations as a result of instability within the business cycle in general) whereby longer-term and sustained opportunities are not available to those who take employment in hotels, as resort couriers or ski instructors. It is also reflective of short-termism within many tourism and hospitality businesses which may be unwilling to seek long-term commitment in return for reciprocal long-term investment in the recruit.

As a consequence, many entrants to the sector do so with assumptions of impermanence-this is work to be undertaken on the way to somewhere else, a first exposure to the demands of the workforce but one to be shed when better opportunities arise elsewhere in the economy. Furthermore, as Riley (1996) shows, the sector is one of unconstrained access to most of its working positions and one which, therefore, benefits from unrestrained recruitment to most of its positions but, conversely, also suffers because the skills it engenders in its workforce are in considerable demand within other areas of the service economy. Thus, while entry is open, so is the opportunity to move out elsewhere, both within tourism and hospitality, and to other employment areas. Staff turnover, therefore, can be very high, especially in tight and competitive labour markets, and is a major inhibitor for organizations and destinations seeking to achieve overall enhancement of service and product quality.

A key issue, relating to recruitment, is that of specific skills shortages in key technical and some managerial areas. In part, this is an extension of the concerns addressed above-image, conditions, remuneration-but is also linked to a reluctance, within some industry sectors and businesses, to invest in the skills development of their key personnel. The Irish tourism industry, throughout a period of sustained growth from the mid-1980s onwards, has experienced acute shortages of key technical personnel, particularly chefs, despite levels of national unemployment considerably above the European Union average (Walsh, 1993).

Contrary trends, however, also raise important issues with respect to recruitment and retention. The combined impact of technology and product substitution in the workplace; centralization of key management functions (finance, information analysis, marketing); standardization of product and service delivery; and delayering of management structures in many developed tourism economies means that opportunities for meaningful and developmental careers in skilled craft or managerial areas have been reduced. Reduced opportunity, in turn, impacts on perceptions of the sector and the likelihood of young people, in particular, opting for tourism/hospitality as their career choice.

A changing tourism and hospitality industry environment is, in a sense, complemented but also complicated by changing social expectations of work (Linney and Teare, 1991) and an increasingly diverse profile of employees (Christensen, 1993). Diversity provides the opportunity to create new working environments and conditions, but demands comprehensive review of traditional practice. A good example of this is the present reluctance of many employees to accept split-shift working and the consequent need for employers to reorganize their work environment accordingly.

Education, training and development, for tourism and hospitality is also, in part, a recruitment issue in that providers of educational and training programmes, particularly within the college and university sector, are influenced by the same perceptual factors as the industry itself. Recruitment standards to vocational programmes for the sector are lower than those to equivalent courses in related professional areas, for example business. Tourism studies are, in a sense, somewhat different from hospitality in this respect in that vocational outcomes are less clearly defined and graduate choice is likely to be rather more eclectic.

There are clear opportunities to use such educational programmes in a rather more general education sense rather than facing clear vocational channelling (Baum, 1996). Ritchie (1993) argues that one key issue is a lack of tourism sector consensus as to the need for sector-specific educational provision. Commitment to ongoing career development of existing employees, within tourism and hospitality, varies greatly and is influenced by the sub-sector and the size of the enterprise (Cooper, 1993). The presence of career development opportunities, however, is likely to exert a considerable influence on the retention of ambitious employees, with potential, within the sector.

Recognition remains relatively limited that human resource development is an important contributor to the delivery of quality products and service, within tourism and hospitality, and that this, in turn, impacts on the level of both new and repeat business achieved by businesses and destinations. This situation has altered significantly in recent years and the business advantage achieved, through a people focus, by companies such as British Airways, Singapore Airlines, Marriott and Ritz Carlton, has been an important contributory factor. However, many small businesses do not have the resources or skills to focus on their human capital. Given that tourism destinations have images that are only as strong as their weakest link, it is important to strive to ensure that the visitor's experience is positive throughout the full range of contact with the providers of goods and services.

Human resource development is, frequently, addressed as a reactive concern within tourism and hospitality, and rarely in a proactive and planned sense. Product and market shifts and developments may be the target of strategic analysis and preparation, but it is not common, within the sector, to find enterprises or wider destination communities putting in place recruitment, education and training in support of such change, whether quantitative (in the sense of increased arrivals numbers) or qualitative (in the sense of new market segments) in advance. Recognition of the lead-time needed to achieve benefit from human resource investment is also limited at both corporate and national levels. The above points represent a complex and inter-related series of issues and concerns which have greater or lesser applicability according to the specific corporate or destination context. What is clear is that these issues feature in an assessment of human resources, within tourism and hospitality, wherever such analysis is undertaken, and that the response to them is frequently fragmented and limited by lack of co-ordination and policy direction. These issues are addressed in the context of two research studies reported here.

An Assessment of the Human Resource Demands of the Tourism and Hospitality Industries

This section is based on the work of Spivack (1997). Her study, using Delphi methodologies, sought to identify and measure gaps between the skills and wider human resource requirements of the tourism and hospitality industries, and the provision made by education and training providers in support of the sector. In addition, the study looks to the future and attempts to identify the educational and training priorities for tourism and hospitality in response to changes within the sectoral and wider socio-economic and political environment. The approach of the study was:

To develop a qualitative methodology, through a consensus model approach, for determining gaps between the output of education and training delivery systems and the current and future needs of employers. Inherent in the premise is a falsifiable theory: there is no relationship between education and training system outputs and the delivery of quality service (Spivack, 1997).

This study brings together two areas of applied policy development which impact significantly on the development of a wider and cogent policy framework for human resource development within tourism and hospitality: first, that of quality service attainment as central to a successful tourism and hospitality sector, and, second, that there is a role which public education and training can play in achieving such quality.

Spivack's study consisted of two components, employing similar methodologies but working with distinct groups in order to verify the approach and to test outcomes in different contexts. The first global survey was based on a sample drawn from international tourism interests, from both the public and private sector, and representing a wide range of sub-sectoral interests and geographical regions. The second component involved a localized study, employing a similar approach and located in a region of Spain. Modified Delphi methods were used for both components, recognizing both the benefits that this approach brings to a qualitative study but also its clear limitations (Witt and Moutinho, 1989). Its advantages include the potential breadth of the study, its internal anonymity the manner in which it permits reflection time for participants and the ability of the approach to tackle complex issues in a balanced manner. Problems relate to the sampling process-the rationale for Delphi is that it draws on expert contributors, but there can be difficulties in defining and identifying appropriate expertise; in maintaining response levels over a number of survey rounds; and in the time commitment demanded of participants.

The global study commenced with 100 participants, drawn on a controlled formula basis from both sectoral and geographical populations to ensure minimum representation within each category. The criteria used for inclusion of participants required that panellists exhibit some or all of the following:

- hold upper-level management positions within their field;
- serve in leadership positions in professional associations related to their field;
- demonstrate familiarity with many different career levels within their sector;
- demonstrate leadership and decision-making skills;
- articulate trends impacting their industry;
- possess familiarity with tourism education and training in their world region.

Selection of the sample was based on access to various databases and directories of international tourism. While there must be clear limitations to this process, the final sample met representation criteria in terms of both sectoral and geographical considerations. Communication was by mail and fax. The response rate to the two rounds of the study showed expected levels of drop-out so that the first round was completed by 66 percent of the 100-member sample and the second round by 44, representing a 44 percent participation rate from the original sample. The local study, based on the Castilla-La Mancha region of Spain, employed the same approach but saw some significant modifications to suit local conditions. Participation criteria were modified to reflect the different level of responsibility of tourism sector leaders at a regional level and, as a result, included rather more members with direct line management responsibility for enterprises or tourism agencies. Geographical considerations related to representation of the five provinces within the region, while the sectors were modified to reflect the structure of the local industry. The sample was 160 and the three rounds of the survey were conducted: first, by face-to-face personal interview; second, using a telephone survey based on a questionnaire resulting from analysis of the first-round outcomes; and, finally, through panel workshops in each of the five provinces, requiring panellists to prioritize the outcome issues relevant to their specific area and to develop regional action plans. Participation in the three rounds was as follows:

- Round 1: 160.
- Round 2: 140, representing a 13 percent drop-off.
- Round 3: 39, representing a 76 percent drop-off from the original sample.

The outcomes of the two studies identified a number of key gaps with respect to the human resource requirements, as articulated by the respondents (both public and private sector) and the skills and knowledge of those recruited into the tourism sector, whether from specialist vocational programmes or through the general education process. The main area of deficiency related to what Baum (1990) describes as soft competences within the sector, those relating to communication (with customers, colleagues and in various languages other than the mother tongue), information (technology-derived, but also analysis and interpretation) and service (marketing-related, understanding customer needs), all of which are attributes which are generic to the sector and, indeed, to services in general.

By contrast, technical ability deficiencies were identified as far less significant within both surveys-there is growing recognition that the diminishing technical demands of the sector (as identified above) can readily be met within the workplace by larger employers, provided soft competences and attitude dimensions are in place.

However, the skills requirements of SMEs remains an issue and it is noteworthy that the local study gave a rather less clear-cut endorsement of this assessment than did the global survey representing larger organizations and interests. In policy terms, this central finding affirms previous research at a more localized level and within the context of specific subsectors and suggests the need for review of public education and training provision for the tourism and hospitality sector in terms of curriculum and, indeed, wider focus and purpose.

The global study also gives an indication of future education and training priorities for tourism and hospitality. Spivack (1997) reports a number of what she calls "skills development issues" derived from anticipated changes within the tourism and hospitality sector, and which the panel consensus process prioritized as central to education and training needs in the future. These were, in rank order:

1. Managers will need to develop more skills in human resource management, particularly in knowing how to build an enthusiastic workforce.
2. With continued internationalization of business, all levels of management will need more training, especially in interpersonal and multicultural skills.
3. Environmental awareness and conservation techniques will become an essential part of tourism education at all levels.
4. The expansion of franchises among transnational firms will accelerate the need for international-level quality of service and skill standards.
5. Public health issues, such as AIDS, that relate to the delivery of tourist products and services will become an essential part of tourism education at all levels.
6. Supervisors will need to learn more high-level management skills such as forecasting and strategic planning.

The local study did not generate significantly different responses from those presented above, with the main emphasis on the growing importance of environmental awareness, business acumen and the enhanced role of enterprises in the education and training of the workforce.

On the basis of this assessment, the study also considered and prioritized key training issues for the future. At an education and training level (Spivack, 1997), these were:

1. Schools of tourism and hospitality management will need to strengthen their curriculum content that deals with business administration skills.
2. Managers will need more training to direct a growing contract-based, part-time and possibly job-sharing workforce.
3. With continued technological change, alternative methods of training and education (such as distance learning, multimedia interactive training, etc.) will markedly replace traditional education.
4. In the future, industry will itself assume increasing responsibility for in-house training of employees at all levels, and rely less on formal education.
5. Employees with formal education in tourism and hospitality management studies generally perform better than colleagues who lack such education.
6. Companies will increasingly encourage and pay for continuing education for their employees to ensure employee commitment and retention.
7. International employee exchange programmes at all levels of employment will become commonplace.

With respect to wider personnel issues, a number of priorities were also identified (Spivack, 1997):

1. Industry will favour hiring employees who have a combination of on-the-job training and formal education.
2. Performance standards, rather than other criteria, will increasingly determine employee compensation and benefits.

3. Groups that have been traditionally been under-represented at management levels in the tourism workforce, such as women, will have a greater role in the future.
4 Changing family lifestyles will require companies to incorporate practices such as work-at-home employees (the virtual office) that lead to a more flexible workforce.
5 Employees will be required to adjust their expectations regarding promotion time-frames, entry-level positions and pay.
6. Corporations downsizing will slow the advancement of employees within their own organizations.
7 To increase the quality of service and better compete in the marketplace, employee incentives, for example, stock options, will become standard for companies.

Spivack's study points to a future which is, in part, already here in that some of the indicators and priorities are already recognized by some sectors of the tourism and hospitality industry, and responses are clearly emerging in the light of such recognition. British Airways' planned reorganization of its personnel base, with a shedding of low-skills employees and the recruitment of a flexible, technology-and language-literate workforce in its place, is one example of this recognition. However, the situation is far from even; while some businesses are in a transition stage and moving towards the future painted by this research, others, especially SMEs are locked in the past in their human resource policies and practices, unable or unwilling to face up to the consequences of the issues addressed earlier in this article.

If the human resource environment predicted by Spivack's study is taken to be a reasonable prognosis for the future, there are significant implications for both tourism enterprises and the wider communities within which they exist. What is implied is the need for a significant mind-shift by those providing leadership within the tourism sector, both public and private, but it also points clearly to the need for changes, at a policy and practice level, within the environment controlled by the wider public sector, both tourism-related and that within the provenience of education, training, employment or other labour market authorities. This leads to the second research study addressed in this article.

Worlds in Different Orbit? Policy Dimensions of Tourism and the Labour Market

At a practical level, tourism education, training and development within the firm and beyond as part of public or private institutional provision, is relatively mature in most developed countries and is an evolving area of activity to communities and countries for which tourism and hospitality activity is rather more new. There is, however, ongoing and, at times, acrimonious debate between providers of tourism and hospitality education and those who see themselves as clients of the system, the industry itself, regarding the relevance, level and focus of education and training (Amoah and Baum, 1997; National Liaison Group for Higher Education in Tourism, 1995).

One of the difficulties for tourism and hospitality education is that it is expected to dance to the tune of a fragmented and heterogeneous sector where there are few commonly defined needs at a technical or knowledge level. The requirements of major airlines, hotel companies or heritage sites are diverse in themselves but are also significantly different from the needs of SMEs across the sector. The sector also draws in players from areas of activity which may, at best, acknowledge a tenuous association with tourism and hospitality and, at worst, fail to see their responsibilities in this area at all-such areas can include national parks, leisure and recreational interests, the finance sector, the security services and parts of the retail sector. One of the consequences of a fragmented public and private sector interest in tourism and hospitality is that there is rarely a clear, single authority with responsibility for the management and direction of education, training and development initiatives in support of the sector. In reality, there is frequently a range of organizations and agencies which have some involvement but also have loyalties and interests which lie out with the domain of tourism and hospitality. Such organizations and providers may include:

- the various industry subsectors and their representative associations;
- national, regional or local tourism development agencies, generally public but also in the private domain;
- public sector agencies or government authorities responsible for areas such as heritage, the environment, marine and other water resources, agriculture, national parks, etc.;
- national or provincial education providers;
- private education providers;
- specialist training agencies, public and private;
- national employment, labour or manpower agencies and their respective government departments;
- social partner organizations such as trade unions.

What is frequently seen as a practical issue, in that education providers may or may not be delivering appropriate curricula to meet industry's needs, is also an issue of policy concern and, in many respects, it is policy shifts that will be required to provide the lead, and assist the sector and the wider community to face up to predicted changes within tourism and hospitality in the future. Amoah's (1997) study is one which seeks to establish the extent to which policy formulation in the area of tourism and hospitality evolves in tandem with, or in isolation from, that applicable within the education, training and development domain. While based on empirical work in Western Europe and similar developed-country contexts, the findings appear to be considerably more widely applicable.

Amoah's study is based on a series of national case studies which were the outcome of local interviews and policy analysis. Amoah postulates that effective linkages between policy formulation and implementation in the tourism and the education/labour market environments are an important building block towards meeting the human resource challenges which Spivack identifies. She argues that this outcome is most effective where specific tourism education policies are articulated and put in place as a result of the convergence of the two supporting policy areas. Amoah has articulated this convergence process through presentation of a conceptual model which places tourism and education/training within a policy conceptual framework (Amoah and Baum, 1997), and identifies some of the key linkages which need to be in place for the effective delivery of tourism education, a delivery which can be fully responsive to the range of future needs identified earlier.

In practice, Amoah's research suggests that few, if any, national or sub-national jurisdictions fully acknowledge the policy linkages which the framework proposes. Indeed, the reality, in many cases, is that the two key policy domains of tourism and education (where both are clearly identifiable) can operate in either virtual isolation or on the basis of dependency and adaptation where tourism and hospitality are required to respond to or accommodate, within policy and practices driven by education and training, priorities developed without specific sectoral reference.

It is arguable, for example, that the NVQ/GNVQ vocational education framework which was developed in the UK in the early 1990s was done so without specific sectoral consideration or recognition of policy priorities within tourism and hospitality.

As a consequence, the structural and content focus does not fully meet tourism and hospitality industry needs. That said, it is difficult to fully verify this argument at a policy level because the UK, in common with many jurisdictions, has little more than embryonic components of a national tourism policy.

Amoah's research points to approaches at a provincial level in parts of Canada and at a national level in the Republic of Ireland as representative of environments where policy convergence is most in evidence and most effectively implemented. In both situations, this policy convergence is achieved under the auspices of a national or provincial co-ordination agency. While commencing life as public sector bodies, a number of the Canadian models-for example, the Alberta Tourism Education Council (ATEC)-have been moved out of the public sector and now operate as private bodies. The Irish model, through CERT:

...is unique (in Europe) in that it provides by far the most comprehensive approach to co-ordinating the inputs of education and the tourism industry into a unified system and, through CERT, operates through total coordination and the identification of training and development needs at both macro and micro levels (Baum, 1995).

What these models have in common is a starting point within identified national and provincial tourism and hospitality policy priorities and the interpretation of these within the context of the education, training and development environment. As a result, modification of the latter is possible and takes place to accommodate sectoral needs. In Ireland, specific tourism and hospitality programmes, operating within different parameters and with divergent objectives to those found in other vocational areas, were developed in the mid-1980s to provide career access within the secondary school system. This initiative, in turn, influenced the structure and focus of a wider system of vocational provision across other curriculum areas-in other words, tourism and hospitality policy requirements impacted on and gave direction to wider vocational educational policy within the country.

5

Housekeeping and Homeland Security Automation

A year after the creation of the Department of Homeland Security, the House leadership ponders whether it needs a permanent committee to oversee the department. The answer is yes.

When the President proposed the Homeland Security Act to Congress, it was referred to 12 standing committees in the House thought to have jurisdiction over the legislation. That was the right thing to do. Domestic security missions touch every federal agency and cut across national programs. Even today, a year after the creation of the Department of Homeland Security, virtually every federal department has responsibilities for protecting the nation.

Safeguarding the lives and property of Americans remains a mission that cuts across the federal executive and correspondingly the committees of Congress. Officials in the Department of Homeland Security will always find themselves—and rightly so—scurrying from committee room to committee room, testifying on their efforts to integrate a plethora of activities into a coherent, integrated national structure of systems and programs.

While security remains a cooperative government effort, we needed a dedicated Homeland Security Department. The rationale for the initiative paralleled the thinking behind the formulation of the 1947 National Security Act, consolidating key assets into one big, powerful organization and creating the means to orchestrate that department's efforts with other federal activities. Large, centralized organizations have drawbacks, the most obvious being the problems encountered in managing a vast bureaucracy. But big organizations can also have great strengths, providing unity of purpose, a wealth of capabilities, and economies of scale, and fostering a common institutional culture and practices that build trust and confidence and facilitate coordinated action.

The department now also faces the same challenges that confronted the Pentagon in 1947. In terms of efficiencies and improved coordination, the low-hanging fruit of corralling over 180,000 employees into one agency has been picked. What is left to be done is the hard work, the nuts and bolts of building a real department—implementing human capital, acquisition, and information technology programs; building security systems that match the national strategy; and standing watch every day against terrorist attacks. Oversight of these activities requires standing committees with the expertise and experience to see the big picture and dig into the details.

The House Select Committee on Homeland Security has already demonstrated that there could be value added in consolidating oversight in a single committee. They've held productive hearings and rapidly assembled a capable staff with the energy, expertise, and dedication that make for good congressional oversight. Last week, the full committee passed out H.R. 3266, Faster and Smarter Funding for First Responders, a necessary piece of legislation and a great example of the kind of leadership needed from a permanent oversight committee.

The global war against terrorism will be a long, protracted conflict. We need a Department of Homeland Security that is built and run to protect Americans today, tomorrow, and ten and twenty years from now. We need a Congress that is properly organized to support this effort. Leaving jurisdiction for the department's homeland security programs fragmented among a dozen committees runs counter to the intent behind the Homeland Security Act of 2002: either merge functions, change cultures, and focus the federal government on homeland security or turn the initiative over to the terrorists.

Safeguarding Assets: Custodianship Responsibilities

One of the major requirements of good internal control is to safeguard assets. In expressing an opinion on the financial statements of an organization, certified public auditors (and governmental auditors) are required to evaluate the system of internal control in place and to determine if reportable conditions exist. A material weakness in internal control related to fixed assets or inventories may lead to a qualified financial statement for the State of Wisconsin or an institution. A more than relatively low level of risk may result in a finding of a reportable condition in the audit report.

Similarly, good business practice requires that assets be appropriately secured and maintained, used for the purposes intended, periodically accounted for, and properly disposed of. Wisconsin Statutes require that the Business Manager ("Steward") of each institution "have immediate charge of all books, accounts, papers, and records relating to the institution's financial management." The Business Manager should also "be responsible for the safekeeping and economical use of all stores and supplies." In addition, section 46.03 requires that the department "supervise, manage, preserve and care for the buildings, grounds and other property pertaining to said institutions, and promote the objects for which they are established."

OMP Uniform Administrative Requirements for Grants and Cooperative Agreements to State and Local Governments ("Common Rule") requires, with respect to equipment, that states are to use, manage and dispose of equipment in accordance with state policies. Federal requirements include maintaining equipment, appropriate records, taking periodic physical inventories, and maintaining an adequate internal control system. Material noncompliance with these requirements may result in a compliance audit finding and/or qualified financial statements. In addition, federal grant agreements may have specific requirements relating to fixed assets and equipment.

Policy

Each Division or Institution shall establish adequate internal control procedures to ensure that fixed assets, equipment and supplies are appropriately safeguarded. These procedures shall include, but not be limited to:

1. Assigning custodianship responsibilities for each asset or type of asset or location;
2. Complying with Department of Administration risk management requirements and due professional care;
3. Maintaining accurate and reliable accounting records for fixed assets and inventories and reconciling fixed asset subsidiary records to FMS records;
4. Conducting an annual (in some cases, biennial) physical inventory of all assets to be reported in the Department's financial statements;
5. Immediately investigating missing equipment and reporting the disappearance in a timely manner to federal, state or local officials, as needed;
6. Disposing of surplus equipment in accordance with state and departmental requirements and/or federal grant requirements and agreements.

Custodianship Responsibilities

Designation of Custodian(s). Custodianship involves the responsibility for safeguarding an asset or group of assets. Each division or institution should designate a custodian for each piece (or each location) of capital equipment. The custodian may be the employee who uses the equipment, the immediate supervisor, the Bureau director, or an employee who is formally assigned division-wide functions. The custodian's responsibilities are to assure that the equipment is properly maintained, to assure that the equipment is used for the purposes intended, and assure that information regarding the equipment is properly reported (acquisitions, transfers, disposals, movements, etc.).

Divisions and Institutions should have a method (preferably in writing) to communicate the responsibilities of custodianship for assets owned by or used by the organization. A custodian is also needed for supplies inventories, including such areas as institution stores inventories, pharmacy inventories, maintenance inventories, food stamp inventories and forms centre inventories. Office supplies may be, for example, under the custodianship of an office manager. A custodian is also needed for all approved petty cash and change funds. Monitoring and Verification. As part of its internal control responsibility, each division and institution needs to monitor custodianship within the organization on a periodic basis. Generally, monitoring and verification is the responsibility of the Business Manager or Management Services Director.

Shared Responsibilities. In an organization as large as DHFS, shared responsibility will be common. For example, pharmacy inventories may be the responsibility of the medical director rather than the Business Manager. In this case, the Legislative Audit Bureau has considered the Business Office responsible for oversight, including explaining inventory variances. Or computer equipment may be owned by one division, used by a subgrantee, and maintained by the Bureau of Information Systems. In this latter case, the division that applied for and received the federal grant is ultimately responsible for the performance of others. Divisions and Institutions need to review the lines of responsibility involving assets and to fix custodianship duties accordingly to ensure proper control regardless of organizational structure.

Risk Management Responsibilities

Due Care and Internal Control. Risk management activities include the proper care for buildings and equipment and adequate protection against fire or theft. In particular, computers must be in rooms with locked doors or secured by cable. Items that are highly portable require additional protection. Such items include laptop computers, video recorders or players, and audiovisual equipment. Thefts are to be reported to the proper authorities. Under federal regulation, adequate maintenance procedures must be developed to keep the property in good condition.

Division and Institutions to ensure adequate safeguards to prevent loss, damage, or theft of the property should develop a control system. Any loss, damage, or theft shall be investigated and properly reported. Periodic risk assessment should be made to determine if proper precautions have been taken within a Division or Institution for the protection of assets. Preventive measures should be taken to limit risk to no more than a relatively low level.

Self-Insurance. The State has a self-insurance program for losses.

Department of Administration requirements should be adhered to, including the reporting of risk management premiums. The Office of Purchasing is the contact for DHFS risk management.

For risk management and property control purposes, a permanent record of all items classified as capital expenditures or major materials and supplies is required. These records form the basis for the Annual Property Coverage Report.

The risk management reports are different from fixed asset and equipment records used in financial reporting. The definition of asset is different, the valuation is different, and the two reports are used for different purposes.

For example, risk management reports are used to determine reimbursement for losses and include all insured property. Fixed asset and equipment records are for capital assets greater than $500 per unit. Risk management valuation is based on an estimate of replacement cost whereas financial accounting records are based on historical, or acquisition cost.

Accurate and Reliable Accounting Records

Separation of duties applies to the safeguarding of assets. Generally, one person should not control a transaction from beginning to end. Division of responsibilities decreases risk. Generally internal control for assets includes three persons:

1. Recordkeeping (including disposals) should be independent of custodianship and the physical inventory to the extent possible.
2. It is preferable, though not required, to have an independent person conduct the physical inventory. Neither the custodian nor the record keeper is independent.

Accounting records are to be updated at least quarterly. Records that are updated once a year after the close of the fiscal year do not provide adequate control. The goal of a double-entry accounting system is to have accurate records as of the end of the month and to enter transactions as they occur.

Currently, DHFS maintains subsidiary systems to record fixed asset and equipment data. Information to be included in the accounting records is detailed in Section 8—Fixed Assets 1.0 (Capital Asset and Inventory Systems). This information is required by federal regulation. Special procedures apply to transfers. All transfers between one DHFS organization and another DHFS organization or another state agency require use of form DMS-476. This information is essential for GAAP reporting purposes and to ensure that a transfer-in is balanced with a transfer-out.

Additions to the subsidiary system records are to be reconciled to FMS records, and the ending balance for the prior year is to be reconciled to the current year's ending balance, annually. These reconciliations are essential to demonstrate that capital assets are being correctly reported and that balances are being carried forward correctly from one year to the next. Any variances should be less than $500 per account.

A physical inventory must be conducted annually (in some cases, BFS may approve biennial physical inventories). Institutions are required by Wisconsin Statutes to perform a physical inventory annually. Results of the physical inventory must be reconciled to the property records and all discrepancies explained.

The physical inventory must be complete and accurate. The Legislative Audit Bureau may interpret any unexplained discrepancies as weak physical control.

Investigation of Missing or Stolen Equipment

Under federal regulation, any loss, damage, or theft shall be investigated promptly. The results of that investigation need to be properly acted upon and reported.

Each item listed as a disposal should be explained as to method of disposal—junked, stolen, missing, transferred, etc. Some software has the capability to record this information by a symbol in the disposal. In all cases, adequate back up information is required as an audit trail.

It is management's responsibility to follow up on any areas where a lack of control is identified in the physical inventory process and to apply corrective action.

Disposal of Equipment

There are a number of requirements for the disposal of equipment. Disposal of equipment is to be done in accordance with state and federal requirements and as well as in compliance with good internal control and accounting procedures, consistent with a state employee's ethical obligations.

Requirements. Section 8—Fixed Assets 5.0: (Disposition of State-Owned Equipment) details most requirements for the disposal of equipment. In addition, there are federal regulations that apply to equipment originally purchased with federal funds, and specific federal grants may have additional conditions. Approval in advance by the DOA Bureau of Procurement must be obtained for the disposal of any piece of equipment with a unit fair market value of greater or equal to $10,000 or have an original purchase price of $10,000 or more. In addition, the Department of Administration requires an annual summary report of equipment disposed of by category.

Internal Controls. All disposal transactions must be consistent with departmental accounting procedures. All receipts from sales must be properly controlled and deposited intact within five working days or less. Generally, the receipts from the sale of surplus property are to be recorded as GPR-Earned or miscellaneous revenue rather than refund of expenditure.

Ethical Considerations. Sales or other disposal of surplus equipment must be in accordance with provisions of the *Employee Handbook,* including, but not limited to, Work Rule #3 (concerning unauthorized use of property), Conflicts of Interest, Use of State Property, and Acceptance of Gifts, Favours or other Renumerations. The appearance of a conflict of interest is to be avoided as well as an actual conflict of interest.

Standards 2.0 (Standards of Business Conduct)

Management Services

The main purpose of MSG is to create and keep valued clients. This can be achieved only if we deliver superior quality. We continually work towards achieving excellence which is a never ending process.

MSG offers the following types of services, directly or indirectly related to housekeeping and other maintenance.

Facility Management Services

- Executive Housekeeping Services
- Support Staff Services
- Floor, Carpet & Upholstery Services.

Facility Management Services

Next to your people, products and services, what's the next most important aspect of your business? The facilities in which it operates. That's why choosing the right partner to maintain, manage and develop your work sites is such a crucial decision. Today, many corporations and government agencies are looking to outsource the management of their corporate or government-owned properties. MSG's experienced professional property managers can assume building management duties, including reconfiguring office space, overseeing build-outs, maintaining HVAC equipment, and supervising security, janitorial, landscaping and other services.

Our Facility Management Services

- Facility Operations & Maintenance
- Executive Housekeeping Services
- Security & Safety Management
- Horticulture Services
- Electrical, Plumbing & Carpentry Services
- D.G. Set Operation & Maintenance
- Pest Control Services

- Heating/Ventilation/Air Conditioning.

Stepping into MSG's Services-maintained and operated facility is a step up.

- A well kept attractive facility greets visitors.
- Employees feel good about their surroundings.
- The company projects a professional image to clients and the public.
- Site passes health, safety and environmental inspections with flying colours.
- Proactive maintenance nips building system problems before they become serious.
- Building systems & equipment operate at peak performance, contributing to efficiency.
- Cost-effective maintenance and use of human resources boost the company's bottom line.

With MSG's Services you get:

- One point of interface.
- Clear-cut responsibility.
- Continuity of service.
- Dedication to the total project.
- and a budget that stays within the boundaries you set.

Executive Housekeeping Services

MSG's housekeeping services are unique due to our depth of understanding of customers' individual needs, and the depth of experience upon which we have built best practices and our company. Our intense housekeeping service training programs, superior on-site management, and the respect we show towards our customers and employees create an environment in which we consistently exceed the janitorial service needs and goals of our clients. Supported by the constant innovation that defines all aspects of MSG quality, our housekeeping services put clients first with advances like the Green Clean program. MSG has the staffing, expertise and understanding required to meet all your housekeeping service needs in a demanding high traffic environment. You can have confidence that day in and day out, MSG's service best practices, will please your customers while making your business shine.

Our Executive Housekeeping Division consists of following services:

- General Cleaning
- Post Construction Cleaning
- High Pressure Cleaning of Outside Areas
- Cleaning of Glass Walls and Curtains
- Cleaning of facade of High Rise Building
- Restroom Cleaning
- Spring Cleaning
- Steam Cleaning Operations
- Hot water Injection Extraction
- Foam Generator for Carpet & Sofa Shampooing.

The material and machines used by us are standardized and 100% environment friendly.

Support Staff Services

By outsourcing office services to MSG, our customers ensure their administrative operations are as streamlined and smooth-running as their physical plant. Document management, mail and distribution, and office support-all play key role in,the successful performance. of business operations. MSG has the staff and expertise to provide a seamless office services solution.

- Front Desk Executives
- ELP Desk Executives
- Data Entry Operators
- Drivers
- Peon
- Pantry Staff and Supplies
- Other Services

- Store Services
- Photocopy and Fax Services
- Document Management Services
- Mail and Distribution Services
- Courier and Message Services
- Interoffice Mail Distribution
- Office Support Services
- Audio/Visual Services
- Secretarial & Clerical Services
- Job Pick-up and Delivery
- Key-Operators
- Office Supplies
- Service Call Desks
- Switch board/Reception.

Floor, Carpet & Upholstery Services

Floor maintenance is an expertise area at MSG. Our technicians are expertly trained to properly and professionally maintain any floor surface, including hardwood, ceramic, marble, epoxy, VCT, carpet, concrete and more. MSG offers the full scope of floor services to its customers. These services include: I. Hardwood: MSG's professionals are expertly trained to repair, and maintain all hardwood floor surfaces. Our experts have extensive knowledge of all factors that affect and contribute to the changing moisture content of wood flooring before, during and after installation. This knowledge, coupled with extensive training in proper techniques of sanding, screening, cleaning and restoration has contributed to MSG's position as the leader.

Whether repairing a "tripping hazard," re-carpeting fitting rooms or sales floors providing an ongoing cleaning program in retail stores or office buildings, MSG's professionals follow specific, detailed service procedures that keep your carpets in optimum condition. III. Ceramic: MSG's staff is trained to properly repair, install, and clean ceramic floors. Knowing the right chemicals and equipment, we restore and maintain ceramic tile on floors and walls. IV. Marble and Stone: Whether cleaning, polishing, or grinding, MSG's professionals are completely prepared to keep marble and stone in pristine condition. Our staff has the experience and knowledge to ensure proper techniques are followed to allow for the maximum quality that stone and marble floors provide. V. Epoxy: Installation and maintenance of epoxy floor surfaces require the expertly trained and skilled professionals that MSG provides.

Pest Control

Pest control refers to the regulation or management of a species defined as a pest, usually because it is perceived to be detrimental to a person's health, the ecology or the economy.

Pest control is at least as old as agriculture, as there has always been a need to keep crops free from pests. In order to maximize food production, it is advantageous to protect crops from competing species of plants, as well as from herbivores competing with humans.

The conventional approach was probably the first to be employed, since it is comparatively easy to destroy weeds by burning them or plowing them under, and to kill larger competing herbivores, such as crows and other birds eating seeds. Techniques such as crop rotation, companion planting (also known as intercropping or mixed cropping), and the selective breeding of pest-resistant cultivars have a long history.

Many pests have only become a problem because of the direct actions of humans. Modifying these actions can often substantially reduce the pest problem. In the USA, raccoons caused a nuisance by tearing open refuse sacks. Many householders introduced bins with locking lids, which deterred the raccoons from visiting. House flies tend to accumulate wherever there is human activity and is virtually a global phenomenon, especially where food or food waste is exposed. Similarly, seagulls have become pests at many seaside resorts. Tourists would often feed the birds with scraps of fish and chips, and before long, the birds would become dependent on this food source and act aggressively towards humans.

In the UK, following concern about animal welfare, humane pest control and deterrence is gaining ground through the use of animal psychology rather than destruction. For instance, with the urban Red Fox which territorial behaviour is used against the animal, usually in conjunction with non-injurious chemical repellents.

Chemical pesticides date back 4,500 years, when the Sumerians used sulfur compounds as insecticides. The Rig Veda, which is about 4,000 years old, also mentions the use of poisonous plants for pest control.

Ancient Chinese and Egyptian cultures are known to have used chemical pest controls. But it was only with the industrialization and mechanization of agriculture in the 18th and 19th century, and the introduction of the insecticides pyrethrum and derris that chemical pest control became widespread. In the 20th century, the discovery of several synthetic insecticides, such as DDT, and herbicides boosted this development. Chemical pest control is still the predominant type of pest control today, although its long-term effects led to a renewed interest in traditional and biological pest control towards the end of the 20th century.

Types of Pest Control

Organic Pest and Insect Control

While chemical pesticides may kill insects effectively, some may also be toxic to human beings and lead to severe environmental degradation if their use is not properly managed. By comparison, natural pesticides, which are usually eco-friendly, are more conducive to environmental sustainability and more beneficial to public wellness. Many species have anti-insect properties but are nontoxic to humans, including *Arisaema jacquemontii,* which has been demonstrated to have an anticancer potency.

Elimination of Breeding Grounds

Proper waste management and drainage of still water, eliminates the breeding ground of many pests. Garbage provides food and shelter for many unwanted organisms, as well as an area where still water might collect and be used as a breeding ground by mosquitoes. Communities that have proper garbage collection and disposal, have far less of a problem with rats, cockroaches, mosquitoes, flies and other pests than those don't. Open air sewers are ample breeding ground for various pests as well. By building and maintaining a proper sewer system, this problem is eliminated.

Poisoned Bait

Poisoned bait is a common method for controlling rat populations, however is not as effective when there are other food sources around, such as garbage. Poisoned meats have been used for centuries for killing off wolves, birds that were seen to threaten crops, and against other creatures.

Field Burning

Traditionally, after a sugar cane harvest, the fields are all burned, to kill off any insects, or eggs, that might be in the fields.

Hunting

Historically, in some European countries, when stray dogs and cats became too numerous, local populations gathered together to round up all animals that did not appear to have an owner and kill them. In some nations, teams of rat catchers work at chasing rats from the field, and killing them with dogs and simple hand tools. Some communities have in the past employed a bounty system, where a town clerk will pay a set fee for every rat head brought in as proof of a rat killing.

Traps

Traps have been used for killing off mice found in houses, for killing wolves, and for capturing raccoons and stray cats and dogs for disposal by town officials.

Poison Spray

Spraying poisons by planes, hand held units, or trucks that carry the spraying equipment, is a common method of pest control. Throughout the United States of America, towns often drive a town owned truck around once or twice a week to each street, spraying for mosquitoes. Crop dusters commonly fly over farmland

and spray poison to kill off pest that would threaten the crops. Many find spraying poison around their yard, homes, or businesses, far more desirable than allowing insects to thrive there.

Destruction of Infected Plants

Forest services sometimes destroy all the trees in an area where some are infected with insects, if seen as necessary to prevent the insect species from spreading. Farms infested with certain insects, have been burned entirely, to prevent the pest from spreading elsewhere.

Effective Way to Control Mosquito Bites

A Complete Guide for Effective Ways to Control Mosquito Bites

Mosquitoes have been in existence for more than 400 million years. The tropical climate is a very pleasant climate for the mosquitoes to survive. The female mosquitoes suck blood from your body for their food. The male mosquitoes feed on flower nectar. The female lays hundreds of eggs at a time. After hatching, the mosquito larva can grow to an adult within 10 days.

Mosquitoes are responsible for various diseases like malaria, dengue etc. If these diseases are not treated properly, they may become fatal. So it becomes essential to prevent these disease carriers from entering your living area. You can control mosquito bites either by restricting the entry of mosquitoes or by killing them.

Stagnant water with moderate summer temperature is favorable for female mosquitoes to lay their eggs. Containers like used bottles, tins, flower pots, garbage cans that hold stagnant water arc loved by mosquitoes. You have to ensure that you don't have stagnant water around your dwelling.

Outdoor Protection

When you have ponds at your outdoor then surely the stagnant water will become a breeding place for mosquitoes. Also when your house is surrounded by thick bushy and marshy woods you have to find some means to control mosquitoes. You can breed mosquito fish, killifish, goldfish or guppies in your pond as they eat mosquito larvae. Frogs and toads are also enemies for mosquitoes.

Indoor Protection

Mosquitoes are present everywhere. You must protect yourself from them by either blocking them from entering your house or killing them as they enter. Many mosquito control products are available in the market and you can use any one of them for your convenience.

Mosquito Sprays

Various mosquito sprays are available in the market that poisons the air sufficient enough to kill the mosquitoes. When you spray these liquids then you can definitely kill all flying mosquitoes. These sprays obviously pollute the air and hence they are dangerous for us too. They don't cause death of human beings but are dangerous especially for kids to inhale them.

Mosquito Repellent Ointment and Coils

Mosquito repellent ointments need to be applied to our parts of the body that are uncovered. They are sometimes greasy and not advisable for children. They effectively repel mosquitoes and hence you can escape from their bites. Coils are effective for use in outdoors. Many people use these coils indoor but they don't kill mosquitoes.

Mosquito Racket Zappers

These rackets are very effective in killing mosquitoes that are flying around you to suck your blood. You have to wave your hands holding these racket zappers and any mosquito that comes in contact with the racket is killed as you press the button to activate the zapper. They use batteries that are rechargeable with some models and replaceable with others.

Electronic Mosquito Killers

These electronic mosquito killers operate in current. They attract the mosquitoes with their ultra violet bulbs and the mosquitoes will be killed as they approach the bulbs surrounded by low voltage grid. They can be used in places that have many mosquitoes.

Mosquito Nets

Mosquito nets are an effective means to protect your small living area. You can cover your bed with hanging nets to prevent mosquitoes from nearing you. These nets are very useful for covering beds where children sleep.

You can also install mosquito nets for your windows and doors to effectively block the entry of mosquitoes. These nets have small holes that are large enough to let the air in and small enough to let the mosquitoes stay out.

Whatever control measures you take you can only control the mosquitoes but you cannot stop their existence. But you must take measures to effectively control mosquitoes in your living area to protect yourself from dangerous diseases.

Electronic Pest Control

Electronic pest control devices use sound waves at certain frequencies, which pests dislike, as a method of controlling pests.

The concept of electronic pest control is relatively new; however, these products have many useful applications. Prior to these new devices, pest control mainly involved using poisons. While the minute amounts of poisons used in pest control may not kill you, they do have the potential of affecting your health adversely on a long-term basis.

The Advantages of Using Electronic Pest Control

There are several advantages of using electronic pest control methods compared to the conventional means of pest control using poisons. In the first place, electronic pest control devices are safe and nontoxic for human beings. Hence, there is no necessity of spraying poisonous stuff in the kitchen and other areas of the house when a simple device, which can just be plugged in, will do the same job quite effectively.

Electronic pest control devices are designed in such a way that the sound wavelengths are only heard by certain insects and do not affect humans at all. Pets are also usually not affected by them. Some of them are designed to affect rodents, hence, if that is the kind you want, you need to check for that. Electronic pest control devices do not kill any insects or animals. The sound waves they produce drive them away without killing them. Hence, you can rest assured of not having to deal with dead bugs all over your home.

One of the best reasons for using an electronic pest control device is that it functions 24/7. Therefore, once it is turned on, you do not need to keep applying any substances every few weeks in order to keep away pests. These systems work day and night without requiring intervention any further.

Each of these devices is effective over a large area, hence, it is recommended to place these units at all entry points of your home. If insects are stopped from coming inside, the problem can be stopped right at the door. While this may be an effective strategy on the ground floor, however, it is advisable to use a device on each floor of the house, since there is no point in allowing pests to hide in some other part of the house.

Various Kinds of Electronic Pest Control Devices

Electromagnetic Pest Control This electronic pest control device is the most interesting and complex. It makes modifications to the wavelengths of the frequency signals that already exist in the wiring of homes, thus agitating rodents and insects. Thus, your entire house is turned into a pest-repelling device by the electromagnetic pest control device, which is the most effective way to keep pests away.

Ultrasonic Pest Control: These are useful for repelling large pests such as rodents from coming into your home. A specific wavelength of sound is used by these which agitate the pests. Humans cannot detect these sound waves, hence this electronic pest control device does not disrupt sleep or any other activity carried out daily. Another plus is that it does not need to be monitored.

Ionic Pest Control: These devices create negative ions which suck out bacteria and fungi from the air. Insects and rodents are also warded off by the negative ions. Although the idea may sound alarming, negative ions occur naturally when there is a storm, hence this device is absolutely safe and will cause no harm to anything but the pests it is intended for.

You can find several pest control calculators on the Internet, which you can use for computing the variables that you input like the amount you want to spend, the kind of pest, the square foot area in order to get the best value for your money. While the ultrasonic pest control device is the most inexpensive type, however, it does not have the air-cleaning feature that the ionic pest control device has. Each of these types of devices has its pros and cons, but all of them are effective for controlling pests.

What to Do if Your Home is Infested with Insects

Find out how awful can some pests be for your house.

At some time, everyone will have pests in their home, it's very hard to keep your house bug free. And when that happens, you need to call an exterminator to remove the pests. There are a lot of types of bugs, which can cause different types of damage. Some are not so bad, while others can be catastrophic. You could try to remove the bugs yourself with a pesticide, but it isn't always as easy as it seems. If you don't do the job properly, you won't get rid of all insects. That's when an exterminator comes in handy.

When you ask a company to check if your house is infested, they will send someone over to inspect it. If the exterminator finds out that you have pests in your home, but doesn't try to properly identify them, he just uses the pesticide, that means he doesn't really know what he is doing. If you don't exactly know what bugs you are infested with you can't choose the best pesticide and the job won't be done properly. For this type work, if it isn't 100% properly done, it's like not doing it at all. That's because not all pests will die and they will regain in numbers after some time.

Probably the worst infestation that can happen to your home is termites. If you don't notice it on time, they can destroy your house worse than an earthquake, storm or fire. That's why you should do a termite inspecting at least once a year. If they are found in time they can be stopped, without causing major damage to your home.

Moles are also bugs that can cause some damage, they like landscapes and lawns a lot. In this case an experimented exterminator will get rid of them very easily. He just has to properly identify the area they live in and then eliminate.

Even if it is very hard to never have bugs in your home you can at least try to prevent it. The best way to do that is to make sure that they have nothing to eat or to drink, because that's what the insects are looking for. Maybe you won't be successful, but the number of insects will surely be lower. If you do nothing about it, the numbers can increase substantially. However the most important thing is to eliminate them properly if they are present, otherwise it's a waste of time!

Pest Control

Indoor enclosed spaces like grow rooms would seem to provide ideal protection to plants against pests and parasites that can cause much harm to crops grown conventionally. It would seem reasonable to believe that since plants are grown in a comparatively sanitized environment without soil, a pest attack scenario would be unlikely, even remote.

But pests wouldn't be pests if they were so easy to shake off; so whether it is a hydroponics grow room or a green house, these tiny and not so tiny marauders have to be kept away. Fortunately, there are several ways growers can go about protecting their precious plants against these invaders.

Anything and everything can serve to introduce pests into the grow room, even humans are no exception. Once pests gain a foothold in the grow room, they multiply manifold, rapidly consuming plants and playing havoc with your indoor garden. The first step to regain control over your grow room is to identify the culprit. Once this is done a number of "soft" and "hard" control options are available to target the offending intruders.

Control Strategies

When only a few plants are infested growers can dip a small brush in insecticide or methylated spirits and apply directly onto plants to eradicate pests such as mealy bug or scale. This method is often very effective in protecting valuable indoor plants where spraying may not be acceptable. Moths can be dealt with using pheromone traps that help eliminate adult moths before they can lay eggs. Even hand-held vacuum cleaners have been reported to be effective against flying pests, particularly whiteflies.

Repellent Sprays, Powders and Formulations

Garlic sprays and hot pepper wax barrier are often used by growers in pest control. While these are mostly available off the shelf at any gardening supplies store, many growers prefer to make their own versions. However, the results seem to be mostly inconsistent, with some growers claiming excellent results while others reporting less than satisfactory outcomes. Some growers report that pests thrive on foliage treated with repellents.

Soaps and Oil Sprays

Soaps and oils have also proved effective in pest control. They work by blocking the pest's breathing pores, thus smothering the pest. They also prevent some pests like mites from moving around and breeding. Soaps and oils are fairly safe. They can be easily stored and conveniently applied. Regular application over long periods, however, leads to buildup of oil/soap on hydroponic system components. This can be washed off from time to time.

Certain mineral compounds and diatomaceous earth work as natural or non-chemical insecticides. Diatomaceous earth has desiccant action on the insects. It also forms an abrasive layer slowing crawling insects like slugs and worms. It forms a dusty residue on hydroponic fruits or vegetables must be washed off.

Biological Formulations

A number of bio-pesticides are available in the market today. Perhaps, the most widely used of these is Bt spray, which is obtained from the bacterium Bacillus thuringinesis. Bt spray is applied to plants which is then absorbed by caterpillars as they feed. A bacterial toxin is formed in the digestive system of the caterpillar, which causes it to stop feeding. Dehydration sets in and the pest dies in a few days. Different strains of Bt have been developed for use against specific insects. It is important to use the right strain of Bt meant for a specific pest as the wrong strain will not work.

Some other products have been formulated from fungal pathogens of various insects. These work best under the right conditions. If the conditions, for example, humidity is not high enough, the controls are not effective.

Botanical Formulations

The two most common botanical extracts used for pest control in hydroponics are a pyrethrum, derived from a daisy (Chrysantehmum Cinaeraefolium) and neem oil derived from the seed kernels of the Indian neem tree (Azadiracta indica).

Pyrethrum is often combined with other compounds to enhance effectiveness; it can be used to control a wide range of pests. Neem oil or various extracts of neem are available as oil, solvent extract and as a ground product. Neem is an insect growth regulator, meaning, it stops the insect's life cycle. Neem is effective on particularly difficult pests like whitefly; it is also a good general purpose spray option for small-scale growers.

Growers often erroneously assume that since they are made with plant extracts soft pesticides are safer than chemical pesticides. The truth is that these can be more toxic to humans than some synthetic pesticides. Handling these products requires the same care and application as synthetic biological controls.

Gardening and Pest Control-Organic or Insecticide?

Need to know what to do when considering natural methods of pest control? A look at the detail with plenty of tips for you to start.

If you are a person that really likes gardening and pest control from time to time, then the tips contained in this article will help you get even more out of your garden. Gardening and pest control is at least as old as agriculture. It's an industry that's growing rapidly. The pest control business has grown more than 50 percent in the last 5 years or so, and nationwide it has become a $7 billion industry.

More and more homes are being built in remote locations. People want to live in the desert or the woods. When you're building in these areas where insects and animals live, it's their home. They only become pests because they come into YOUR home.

What is Gardening and Pest Control?

It's basically the reduction or eradication of pests. Whereas structural pest control is the control of household pests and wood-destroying pests and organisms or such other pests which may invade households or structures, gardening and pest control tends to be the control of pests that are affecting your plants, lawn and/or soil. That can sometimes spill over into the house as well, but by and large, it's the garden we're talking about here. In order to protect our growing areas as well as our health, proper gardening and pest control is a necessity. It is often ignored until pests and their damage are discovered or it has got out of hand. Well there are measures you can take to help eradicate the problem.

How do we Control Pests in the Garden?

Many people see gardening and pest control as a do-it-yourself job. Well that's fair enough-up to a point. Gardening pest control is like visiting the doctor: to prescribe effective treatment your physician must correctly diagnose the problem and determine the extent of the injury as well as the potential for further injury. In surveys, it's been found that many householders don't bother to read the instructions carefully or feel the need to vary the instructions 'because they feel they know better'. That leads to over-concentrated doses of insecticide for example which could be hazardous to your health and any visitors. Of course we are specifically referring to chemicals, as chemical pest control is still the predominant type of pest control today. However, that said, the long-term effects of chemicals has led to a renewed interest in traditional and biological pest control towards the end of the 20th century.

For those who don't do DIY gardening and pest control, there is the option of monthly visits from your local pest control company. One advantage to monthly pest control is that someone should be looking at your house and garden for pest problems regularly. One disadvantage of monthly pest control is that homeowners insist that PCOs apply a chemical treatment monthly whether there is a pest problem or not! The facts of pesticide use in the home and garden are very surprising:

- Each year 67 million pounds of pesticides are applied to lawns.
- Suburban lawns and gardens receive far heavier pesticide applications per acre than most agricultural areas.

Think before you spray a pesticide. You may kill the insects that are heping you keep pests in check. This means you will have to spray more in the future. Also, insects benefit your garden by pollinating your plants, helping them grow and propagate. Don't use persistent, broad-spectrum, contact insecticides like diazinon, malathion and carbaryl. These provide only temporary pest control and are likely to kill more of the natural enemies than the pests. When their enemies are gone, pest populations may soar and become more of a problem than before they were sprayed.

Most consumers also don't realize how potentially harmful they can be:

- Children are particularly vulnerable to pesticides, and the most likely to be exposed to lawn pesticides. Children living in homes that use pesticides (indoor or outdoor) are at a higher risk for developing asthma, lymphoma, childhood leukemia and brain cancer.
- Garden chemicals harm the environment. The US Geological Survey routinely finds every type of garden chemical-particularly weed killers-in the streams and rivers around urban centers.

It's an eye-opening shock isn't it? Can we really, really not be without these methods of pest control?

Gardening and Natural Pest Control

We believe the logical approach to gardening and pest control is to create a balance of organisms in your yard or garden. Natural pest control is less expensive than buying and applying pesticides, and it's safer for your garden, natural wildlife and the environment.

Let's look at some hints and tips to help your gardening and pest control:

- Physical controls like traps, barriers, fabric row covers, or repellants may work for pests
- If a plant, even a tree, has insect pest or disease problems every year, it's time to replace it with a more tolerant variety, or another type of plant that doesn't have these problems.
- By preventing pests from reaching your plants, you can avoid the damage they cause. And in cases where you only see a few pests, physically removing them can often keep the problem under control.

Let's also look at some useful bugs you want to encourage in your garden:

- Assassin bug
- Beneficial nematode
- Bumble bee
- Damselfly
- Ground beetle
- Honey bee
- Mason bee
- Parasitic wasp
- Soldier beetle
- Spider.

Use these tips to make dealing with gardening and pest control a lot easier. If you follow the basics you will virtually eliminate your problem of garden pests forever.

Linen

Linen is a textile made from the fibres of the flax plant, *Linum usitatissimum*. Linen is labour intensive to manufacture, but when it is made into garments, it is valued for its exceptional coolness and freshness in hot weather. It is superior to cotton in this regard.

Textiles in linen weave pattern made of cotton, hemp and other non-flax fibres may also be loosely, if improperly, referred to as "linen". Such fabrics generally have their own specific names other than linen, for example, fine cotton yarn in linen weave is called Madapolam.

The collective term linens is still often used generically to describe a class of woven and even knitted bed, bath, table and kitchen textiles. The name linens is retained because traditionally, linen was used for many of these items. In the past, the word "linens" was also used to mean lightweight undergarments such as shirts, chemises, waistshirts, lingerie, and detachable shirt collars and cuffs, which were manufactured almost exclusively of linen.

Linen textiles appear to be some of the oldest in the world: their history goes back many thousands of years. Fragments of straw, seeds, fibres, yarns, and various types of fabrics which date back to about 8000 B.C. have been found in Swiss lake dwellings. Linen was used in the Mediterranean in the pre-Christian age. Linen was sometimes used as currency in ancient Egypt. Egyptian mummies were wrapped in linen because it was seen as a symbol of light and purity, and as a display of wealth. Some of these fabrics, woven from hand spun yarns, were extremely fine, and cannot be matched by modern spinning techniques.

Today linen is usually an expensive textile, and is produced in relatively small quantities. It has a long "staple" (individual fiber length) relative to cotton and other natural fibres.

Flax Fiber

Flax fibres vary in length from about 25 to 150 centimeters (18 to 55 in) and average 12-16 micrometers in diameter. There are two varieties: shorter tow fibres used for coarser fabrics and longer line fibres used for finer fabrics. Flax fibres can usually be identified by their "nodes" which add to the flexibility and texture of the fabric.

The cross-section of the linen fiber is made up of irregular polygonal shapes which contribute to the coarse texture of the fabric.

Properties

Highly absorbent and a good conductor of heat, linen fabric feels cool to the touch. Linen is the strongest of the vegetable fibres, with 2 to 3 times the strength of cotton. It is smooth, making the finished fabric lint free, and gets softer the more it is washed. However, constant creasing in the same place in sharp folds will tend to break the linen threads. This wear can show up in collars, hems, and any area that is iron creased during laundering. Linen has poor elasticity and does not spring back readily, explaining why it wrinkles so easily.

Linen fabrics have a high natural luster; their natural colour ranges between shades of ivory, ecru, tan, or grey. Pure white linen is created by heavy bleaching. Linen typically has a thick and thin character with a crisp and textured feel to it, but it can range from stiff and rough, to soft and smooth. When properly prepared, linen fabric has the ability to absorb and lose water rapidly. It can gain up to 20% moisture without feeling damp.

When freed from impurities, linen is highly absorbent and will quickly remove perspiration from the skin. Linen is a stiff fabric and is less likely to cling to the skin; when it billows away, it tends to dry out and become cool so that the skin is being continually touched by a cool surface. It is a very durable, strong fabric, and one of the few that are stronger wet than dry. The fibres do not stretch and are resistant to damage from abrasion. However, because linen fibres have a very low elasticity, the fabric will eventually break if it is folded and ironed at the same place repeatedly.

Mildew, perspiration, and bleach can also damage the fabric, but it is resistant to moths and carpet beetles. Linen is relatively easy to take care of, since it resists dirt and stains, has no lint or pilling tendency, and can be dry cleaned, machine washed or steamed. It can withstand high temperatures, and has only moderate initial shrinkage.

Linen should not be dried too much by tumble drying: it is much easier to iron when damp. Linen wrinkles very easily, and so some more formal linen garments require ironing often, in order to maintain perfect smoothness. Nevertheless the tendency to wrinkle is often considered part of the fabric's particular "charm", and a lot of modern linen garments are designed to be air dried on a good hanger and worn without the necessity of ironing.

A characteristic often associated with contemporary linen yarn is the presence of "slubs", or small knots which occur randomly along its length. However, these slubs are actually defects associated with low quality. The finest linen has very consistent diameter threads, with no slubs.

Measure

The standard measure of bulk linen yarn is the lea. This is a specific length, or indirect grist system, i.e. the number of length units per unit mass. A yarn having a size of 1 lea will give 300 yards per pound. The fine yarns used in handkerchiefs, etc. might be 40 lea, and give 40x300 = 12,000 yards per pound. The symbol is NeL. More commonly used in continental Europe is the Metric system, Nm. This is the number of 1,000 m lengths per kilogram.

In China, the English Cotton system unit, NeC, is common. This is the number of 840 yard lengths in a pound.

Production Method

The quality of the finished linen product is often dependent upon growing conditions and harvesting techniques. To generate the longest possible fibres, flax is either hand-harvested by pulling up the entire plant or stalks are cut very close to the root. After harvesting, the seeds are removed through a mechanized process called "rippling" or by winnowing.

The fibres must then be loosened from the stalk. This is achieved through retting. This is a process which uses bacteria to decompose the pectin that binds the fibres together. Natural retting methods take place in tanks and pools, or directly in the fields. There are also chemical retting methods; these are faster, but are typically more harmful to the environment and to the fibres themselves.

After retting, the stalks are ready for "scutching", which takes place between August and December. Scutching removes the woody portion of the stalks by crushing them between two metal rollers, so that the parts of the stalk can be separated. The fibres are removed and the other parts such as linseed, shive, and tow are set aside for other uses. The short fibres are separated with heckling combs by 'combing' them away, to leave behind only the long, soft flax fibres.

After the fibres have been separated and processed, they are typically spun into yarns and woven or knit into linen textiles. These textiles can then be bleached, dyed, printed on, or finished with a number of treatments or coatings.

An alternate production method is known as "cottonizing" which is quicker and requires less equipment. The flax stalks are processed using traditional cotton machinery; however, the finished fibres often lose the characteristic linen look.

Producers

Flax is grown in many parts of the world, but top quality flax is primarily grown in Western Europe. In very recent years bulk linen production has moved to Eastern Europe and China, but high quality fabrics are still confined to niche producers in Ireland, Italy and Belgium.

Uses

Over the past 30 years the end use for linen has changed dramatically. Approximately 70% of linen production in the 1990s was for apparel textiles whereas in the 1970s only about 5% was used for fashion fabrics.

Linen uses range from bed and bath fabrics (tablecloths, dish towels, bed sheets, etc.), home and commercial furnishing items (wallpaper/wall coverings, upholstery, window treatments, etc.), apparel items (suits, dresses, skirts, shirts, etc.), to industrial products (luggage, canvases, sewing thread, etc.). It was once the preferred yarn for handsewing the uppers of moccasin-style shoes (loafers), but its use has been replaced by synthetics. A linen handkerchief, pressed and folded to display the corners, was a standard decoration of a well-dressed man's suit during most of the first part of the 20th century.

Currently researchers are working on a cotton/flax blend to create new yarns which will improve the feel of denim during hot and humid weather.

Linen fabric is one of the preferred traditional supports for oil painting. In the United States cotton is popularly used instead as linen is many times more expensive there, restricting its use to professional painters. In Europe however, linen is usually the only fabric support available in art shops. Linen is preferred to cotton for its strength, durability and archival integrity.

In the past linen was also used for books (the only surviving example of which is the Liber Linteus). Due to its strength, in the Middle Ages linen was used for shields and gambeson (among other roles such as use for a bowstring), much like how in Classical antiquity and Hellenistic Greece linen was used to make multiplied Hoplite cuirasses. Also because of its strength when wet, Irish linen is a very popular wrap of pool/billiard cues, due to its absorption of sweat from hands. Paper made of linen can be very strong and crisp, which is why the United States and many other countries print their currency on paper that is made from 25% linen and 75% cotton.

History

Linen has been used for table coverings, bed coverings and clothing for centuries. The exclusivity of linen stems from the fact that it is difficult and time consuming to produce (flax in itself requires a great deal of attention in its growth). Flax is difficult to weave because of its lack of elasticity, and therefore is more expensive to manufacture than cotton. The benefits of linen however, are unmatched.

The Living Linen Project was set up in 1995 as an Oral Archive of the knowledge of the Irish linen industry still available within a nucleus of people who were formerly working in the industry in Ulster. There is a long history of linen in Ireland.

The use of linen for priestly vestments was not confined to the Israelites, but from Plutarch, who lived and wrote one hundred years after the birth of Christ, we know that also the priests of Isis wore linen because of its purity.

In December 2006 the General Assembly of the United Nations proclaimed 2009 to be the International Year of Natural Fibres, so as to raise the profile of linen and other natural fibres.

Antiquity

When the tomb of the Pharaoh Ramesses II, who died 1213 BC, was discovered in 1881, the linen wrappings were in a state of perfect preservation-after more than 3000 years. In the Belfast Library there is preserved the mummy of "Kaboolie,' the daughter of a priest of Ammon, who died 2,500 years ago. The linen on this mummy is in a like state of perfection. When the tomb of Tutankamen was opened, the linen curtains were found intact.

Earliest Linen Industry

In olden days, in almost every country, each family grew flax and wove the linen for its own use; but the earliest records of an established linen industry are 4,000 years old, and come to us from Egypt. The earliest written documentation of a linen industry comes from the Linear B tablets of Pylos, Greece, where linen is depicted as an ideogram and also written as "ri-no" (Greek: *linon*), and the female linen workers are catalogued as "ri-ne-ja" (*lineia*).

The Phoenicians, who, with their merchant fleet, opened up new channels of commerce to the peoples of the Mediterranean, besides developing the tin mines of Cornwall, introduced flax growing and the making of linen into Ireland before the birth of Christ, but the internal dissensions, which even in those early days were prevalent in Erin, militated against the establishment of an organized industry, and it is not until the twelfth century that we can find records of a definite attempt to systematize flax production.

When the Edict of Nantes was revoked, in A.D. 1695, many of the Huguenots who had to flee the country settled in the British Isles, and amongst them was Louis Crommelin, who was born, and brought up as a weaver of fine linen, in the town of Cambrai.

He fled to Ulster, and eventually settled down in the small town of Lisburn, about ten miles from Belfast.

During the late war Cambrai became well known as one of the centers of the most desperate fighting. The name "cambric" is derived from this town.

Although the linen industry was already established in Ulster, Louis Crommelin found scope for improvement in weaving, and his efforts were so successful that he was appointed by the Government to develop the industry over a much wider range.than the small confines of Lisburn and its surroundings. The direct result of his good work was the establishment, under statute, of the Board of Trustees of the Linen Manufacturers of Ireland in the year 1711.

Religion

In the Jewish religion, the only law concerning which fabrics may be used together in clothing regards the mixture of linen and wool. This mixture is called *shaatnez* and is clearly restricted in Deuteronomy 22:11 "Thou shalt not wear a mingled stuff, wool and linen together" and Leviticus 19:19, "'...neither shall there come upon thee a garment of two kinds of stuff mingled together.'" There is no explanation for this in the Torah and is categorized as a type of law known as *hukim*, a statute beyond man's ability to comprehend.

Some Christians believe that it is because God hates mixture and confusion of any kind, similar to having two different animals yoked together and sowing different seed in the same field.

Linguistic Note

The word linen is derived from the Latin for the flax plant, which is *linum*, and the earlier Greek *linon*. This word history has given rise to a number of other terms:

- line, derived from the use of a linen thread to determine a straight line;
- liniment, due to the use of finely ground flax seeds as a mild irritant applied to the skin to ease muscle pain

- lining, because linen was often used to create a lining for wool and leather clothing
- lingerie, via French, originally denotes underwear made of linen
- linseed oil, an oil derived from flax seed
- linoleum, a floor covering made from linseed oil and other materials.

In addition, the term in English, *flaxen-haired,* denoting a very light, bright blonde, comes from a comparison to the colour of raw flax fiber.

Fabrics Types

Kitchen and table linens are made of variety of fabrics. Fabrics are such that they suit the requirements and purpose of the linens. Fabrics with quality and protective properties are widely used for the purpose.

Following types of fabrics are used for making table and kitchen linen:

- Cotton Fabric
- Linen Fabrics
- Hemp Fabric.

Cotton Fabric

Cotton Fabric is noted for its versatility and its natural comfort. Cotton cloth has been used since primitive ages dating back to about 3000 B.C. Today, the main uses of cotton is in the form of garments, home furnishings, and industrial cloths. Cotton fabric undergoes various finishing processes to meet specific end use requirements. Cotton table and kitchen linens are available in numerous designs and styles and in a rainbow of colours. Innovative patterns are either embroidered or printed or painted on these linens to make them look even more beautiful.

Characteristics of Cotton Fabric

- Comfortable
- Soft hand

- Absorbent
- Absorbs and release perspiration quickly
- Can stand high temperatures
- Good colour retention, prints well
- Machine-washable, dry-cleanable
- Good strength
- Easy to handle and sew
- Flame retardant
- Pleasant matte luster
- Good elasticity.

Types of Cotton Weaves

- Diaper Cloth is a twill, dobby or plain woven absorbent cotton.
- Dimity is sheer, thin, white or printed fabric with lengthwise cords, stripes or checks.
- Drill is a strong twilled cotton fabric, used in men's and women's slacks.
- Duck is a heavy, durable tightly woven fabric. Heavy weight drill is used in awnings, tents, etc. Lighter duck is used in summer clothing.
- Flannel cotton is plain or twill weave with a slight nap on one or both sides.
- Flannelette is a soft cotton fabric with a nap on one side.
- Gauze is a sheer, lightly woven fabric similar to cheesecloth. Is also made in silk.
- Gingham is a lightweight, washable, stout fabric that is woven in checks, plaids or stripes.
- Lawn is a plain weave, soft, very light, combed cotton fabric with a crisp finish.

Care of Cotton Fabric

- Cotton can be easily laundered. It can withstand high temperatures.

- Any good detergent can be used to wash cotton.
- It requires frequent pressing as it wrinkles easily.
- Cotton can be ironed with a hot iron, and does not scorch easily.

Linen Fabrics

Linen is noted to be the most luxurious, comfortable and elegant fabric. It is a fabric mad from avegetable fiber called flax. Flax is a bast fiber taken from the stalk of the plant. The luster is from the natural wax content.

Linen has long been used for making decorative and functional table cloths and napkins. Linen is the strongest fabric even stronger than cotton. Apart from being a strong fabric it is also lint free and is used for various purposes.

Characteristics of Linen Fabrics

- Comfortable
- Good strength, twice as strong as cotton
- Hand-washable or dry-cleanable
- Crisp hand
- Tailors well
- Absorbent
- Dyes and prints well
- Lightweight to heavyweight
- No static or pilling problems
- Fair abrasion resistant
- Good conductor of heat
- High tensile strength.

Types of Linen Weaves

- Damask : It is a jacquard weave, is a reversible rich weave, patterned in satin or plain weave.
- Venise : It is a very fine damask table linen consisting of large floral patterns.

Care of Linen Fabrics

- Linens can be hand washable but some are recommended to be dry cleaned especially decorative linen.
- White linens should be dried in the sun, if to help them to keep their whiteness.
- Linen just loves to be washed and ironed. The more linen is washed the softer, nicer and shinier it becomes.
- If the water you use is hard due to a high lime content add a softening agent, especially for darker-colored articles. Use plenty of water because linen is very water-absorbent.
- Do not soak, boil off, rub or wring out embroidered articles.
- Linen is best stored in a cool, dry and well-ventilated area.
- Linen fabrics may need frequent pressing, unless treated for crease resistance.

Hemp Fabric

Hemp is a soft and a warm fabric made from a bast fiber of a plant. Hemp fabric is obtained from the stems of the plant. The stems of the plant are processed to dissolve the gum or the pectin found in it. The fiber is then separated and again processed. After the processing is over, it is woven into yarns and fabric. The finest hemp fabric is produced in Italy. China is the world's leading producer of hemp.

The valued primary fibres are contained around the hollow, woody core of the hemp stalk. These are converted into beautiful apparel and decoratives. Hemp make goods table and kitchen linen because of its durability.

Characteristics of Hemp Fabric

- Durable and strong
- Absorbent
- Naturally resistant to mold, mildew, rot
- High heat conductivity
- Low elasticity
- Beautiful luster

- High affinity for dyes
- Good abrasion
- Softens with each washing, without fiber degradation
- Breathable.

Care of Hemp Fabric

- It should be washed with warm water.
- It should not be washed with bleach as bleach may weaken the surface.
- It is naturally mothproof and so can be stored easily.
- Avoid drying cupboards which have heated pipelines running through because it may discolor hemp.
- Use a dye free detergent with satin lifter.

Wedding Table Linen

Wedding table linens can enhance any table setting at the wedding and protect the tables. These table linens are usually white and are placed on the tables with decorative accessories like napkin holder, flower vases, etc. These linens complete the overall theme and atmosphere for the meal. They are also perfect for bridal shower or luncheon.

Wedding Table Linen Fabric

The most common fabrics used for wedding table linens include:

- Cotton Wedding Table Linen : Cotton is a cool, soft, comfortable and the principal table linen fiber.
- Silk Wedding Table Linen : Silk fabric has a soft, lustrous and a supple hand. Silk table linens are common at royal and luxurious weddings.
- Satin Wedding Table Linen : At times satin is also used for the purpose. It is a thick cloth with a glossy surface.

Napkins

Table and kitchen linens are incomplete without napkins. Napkins are a must-have item in your kitchen. Similarly, a dining table with its runner, placemats, and cover looks slightly empty without napkins. Whether to wipe your hands, face, cleaning utensils, napkins are a multipurpose table linens. At the same time, napkins if properly folded give an enhanced look to your entire dining room setup. A large variety of decorative and designer napkins are perfect in terms of maintaining hygiene and adding glitter to household.

Designs

The beautiful napkins are available in a wide varieties of designs and can be custom-designed in accordance with the specifications and demands of different customers. They add a welcome touch of cheer and soft colour to casual table settings.

Types of Napkins

Attractive napkins are made of various materials like:

- Cotton Napkins
- Linen Napkins
- Paper Napkins.

Table Clothes

Tablecloth can give a distinct look to your dining area. Cotton tablecloths have been handed down from generation to generation.

Designs

Available in a huge medley of pleasing colours and sizes, the collection of cotton tablecloth is extremely appealing and beautifully compliment the look of the room. These table clothes can also be easily dyed and the colour does not fade when washed. They are made using contemporary and traditional designs. In some case, the table clothes can be reversible. There are hand woven cotton table cloths which give a very ethnic look.

Patterns

Cotton tableclothes may be embellished with different kinds of decoration techniques including embroidery, applique work, hand-painting, printing etc. They may have a host of interesting patterns that include paisleys, florals, animals, check, stripes, geometric and abstract prints.

Doilies

Doilies are ornamental table mats placed underneath a dish or bowl or any decorative piece. Doilies provide a beautiful decorative touch to any table, whether a dining table, a coffee table, side table or any other table. Table Doilies are very useful table linens which can protect your furniture from scratches from crockery. Doilies can be used for various in variety of ways depending on the size. These can be used as table mats, coasters, runners, table covers as well as chair covers. Doilies are made using crochet or knitting techniques.

Designs of Doilies

Usually all doilies are crocheted ones having beautiful snowflake designs and available in variety of shapes and colours and diameters. All shabby chic doilies are made of crotchet thread like cotton thread, woolen thread, linen threads and look great on any table. There are crocheted doilies with embroidery on the centre cloth and crocheted lace in the periphery. This gives a fantastic look on the entire table. Openwork of the doilies allows the table surface to show through. In addition to their decorative function, doilies have a utilitarian role, protecting fine wood furniture from scratches.

Table Covers

Table covers have gained immense popularity as a luxury cum necessity. Table covers are made of various materials like cotton, linen, denim and other fabrics. Cotton Table covers are high in demand and are skillfully woven as perfect compliments for sophisticated tables and thus, give an impeccable appearance to the decor. The diverse patterns, textures and styles in cotton and other table covers with excellent colour combinations are a delight to watch.

Designs

The explicit collection of cotton table covers appeals the

onlooker with its huge variety. The highly distinct designs are always lucrative and eye catching. Cotton table covers can also be custom-designed in accordance with the specifications and demands of the customers.

Variety

The table covers may often be beautifully decorated with moderate beadwork, applique work, hand/machine embroidery. Beautiful embroidery on cotton is used to adorn the table covers, making them ideal for use on festive occasions.

Table Mats/Placemats

When we talk about table decoration, half the task is completed through the right selection of table mats or placemats. Table Mats give the table an accent and decide the dining mood. Thes table mats are available in traditional as well as contemporary patterns and their length varies from 12 to 40 inches. Table mats serve as great tools towards building an appealing decor. They are beautiful accessories that serve as pretty adornments for the tables. Place mats provide the dining area with a multitude of colours, patterns and textures and offer ways to enjoy every meal complimented with a genuine appreciation of creativity.

Materials used

Table mats are made of various materials like jute, plastic, paper, straw, cotton, linen etc. For more durability, linen and cotton table mats are very popular.

Designs & Patterns

Right from trendy styles to classically designed patterns, the impressive collection includes plethora of innovative designs in table mats.

Durable and longlasting, the cotton table mats add a special ambiance to the decor. Table mats usually come in rectangle shape. Howvere, different shapes and sizes with vibrant colour combinations are also available. They may have a host of interesting patterns that include paisleys, florals, geometric and various abstract prints.

Coasters

A coaster is a type of small mat placed under a vessel to protect a tabletop or other surface beneath.

Coasters prevent table finishes from heat damage due to warm dishes and hence not only a decorative table accent but also functional.

Table Coasters are made of various materials like jute, wood, straw, plastic and any fabric like cotton and linen. Cotton coaters are very popular. Linen and cotton coasters can also be padded to makde them thick and heat resistant.

Types of Coasters

The coasters made of fabric like cotton are available in a wide range of styles that include:

- Hand-woven
- Hand painted
- Embroidered
- Machine printed.

Shapes

Perfect for formal entertaining or as an attractive accent for tables, coasters come in a multitude of shapes like:

- Square
- Rectangle
- Triangle
- Round
- Oblong.

Designs

Coasters, especially the cotton ones are available in huge choice of colours and shapes. Designs and patterns are given form using various techniques such as are embroidery, fabric-painting, applique work etc. Manufacturers of table linens have introduced a wide range of spell binding coasters that have long been appreciated for their beauty and designs.

Cheese Cloth

Cheese cloth is a very handy kitchen linen. Made of high density cotton fibre it is a multipurpose linen. It can be used both for domestic as well as commercial purpose.

Types of Cheese Cloth

- Fine Cheese Cloth-Used to drain soften cheese, yogurt, and butter.
- Coarse Cheese Cloth-Used for draining curd, lining cheese shaping moulds and cheese press.

Characteristics of Cheese Cloth

- Made up of high quality woven cotton
- It is washable
- It is reusable.

Applications of Cheese Cloth

- Basting
- Poaching
- Stuffing poultry
- Canning
- Straining
- Wrapping cottage cheese
- Wine making
- Hanging curd.

Tea Towels/Dish Towels

A tea towel is a cloth for drying dishes and is also known as a dish towel. It is very handy and helps to give a neat and clean look to the kitchen. Few tea towels are too lovely to be hidden away. The attractive patterned linen or cotton tea towels are appealing to eyes and also have a high utility.

Characteristics of Tea Towels

- Generally made of an absorbent material.

- Can also be made of high quality paper made of compressed fibre.
- It draws moisture through direct contact using a rubbing motion.

Uses of Tea Towels

- Can be used domestically to clean surfaces and dishes in Kitchen.
- Can be used commercially in Restaurants and Hotels.

Kitchen Linen Products

Kitchen linen are basic necessities which are not only fashionable but also functional. Kitchen linens comprising a wide variety of products like towels, aprons, mittens, pot holders etc. are practical, functional and stylish to make yourself comfortable in a harsh, hot, rigorous environment of your kitchen. These linens are always meant to be beautiful and decorative and also handy. They create a perfect silhouette to any kitchen and add a final touch of elegance which you and your guests will both see and feel. Kitchen linens are a kitchen essentials that add to the kitchen decor through their creative and decorative styles. These linens are manufactured in different sizes for different purposes and can also be made customized.

Materials Used

Some popular fabrics used in the making of kitchen linens are as follows:

- Cotton
- Cotton blends
- Poly tissue
- Silk
- Jute
- Rayon
- Polyester
- Satin

- Organza.

However, of all the materials mentioned above, cotton and linen are the best material options.

Properties of Kitchen Linen Fabrics

Kitchen linen fabrics should be:

- Washable
- Heat resistant
- Absorbent
- Durable
- Machine washable
- Should be perfect for drying utensils and wet hands. Kitchen linens should always be kept handy for use and cleaned regularly for hygiene and tidiness.

Designs and Styles

Kitchen linens are available in an wide array of colours and designs. The cheerful colours and patterns of the linens add a little zing to the tedious work and add a dash of fashionable touch to the kitchen. The linens can be plain or printed. The printed designs can be floral, abstract prints, animal prints, polka dots, checks and stripes, multicolored bold stripes, laces at the borders, sequin, printing, patchwork and many more. They may be embroidered or appliqu? for an unique look. There are many innovative patterns and the choice is endless. The designs of the kitchen linen vary from product to product. They also depend upon their purpose and utilization.

Demand of Kitchen Linen

For creating a happy mood, special ambiance and real aesthetic delight to the kitchen, the kitchen linens are highly demanded in the market. There has been an ever increasing demand for beautiful varieties of table and kitchen linens. According to a recent estimate, these kitchen linens contribute to anywhere from 5 to 10% of the total industry sales all over the world. There is rising demand from US and European countries. And in an attempt to cater to these ever growing demands, manufacturers and exporters are continuing to experiment, and implement new ideas, methods and techniques to acquire a more fashion-oriented design that appeals to International buyers. The customer's preferences for the overall designs and colours of kitchen linens change with the changing seasons or approaching festivals.

Types of Kitchen Linen

Various types of kitchen linens are as follows:

Aprons

Apron is a garment, usually fastened in the back and worn over all or part of the front of the body to protect clothing. They are skillfully crafted out of linen, cotton, denim and other fabrics. These aprons mostly have very large and decorative pockets and a waist band.

The simple style of aprons, fashioned from a rectangular piece of linen or cotton fastened to the waist with either fabric ties or belt, allows for a variety of uses. It protects one's clothing from outer soiling and acts as a gathering basket, as well as a cleaning cloth.

Cooking is not the only time when an apron is handy. It can be used for a variety of jobs that call for a cover up. Physically laborious, dirty and dangerous work requires an apron for protection. Today, cotton aprons have even made their way to the fashion runway when the so-called-new apron dress is made fashionable. Most restaurants require aprons for their workers: host, server and cook. At home, the standard barbecue apron, genderless and simple, is still used to protect one's clothes from grease splatters and floury messes.

The basic style of apron, whether a waiter's half apron or a barbecue apron, has come full circle from its beginning. Initially used for protection in work, the apron has come again to being used, primarily, for occupational demands. While the decorated linen apron has passed in and out of popularity, it seems to be coming back into fashion.

Designs

The explicit collection of aprons has always been in vogue. The huge variety owing to the highly distinct designs are always appealing and eye-catching. Aprons can also be custom-designed in accordance with the specifications and demands of different customers. The cotton aprons are very much in demand because they are easily washable, durable and available in variety of prints and colours.

Pot Holders

Pot holder is a must-have item in the kitchen. A potholder is a small fabric pad which is used to handle hot cooking utensils. Cotton potholders are widely in use because these pot holders are highly durable and can withstand multiple washes and ironing at the highest temperature. The colours also stay sharp. They are capable of rapidly absorbing and yielding moisture and provide plenty of insulation that helps in heat resisting. Made to coordinate with the oven mitten, apron, table runner and place mats, the linen or cotton pot holders are skillfully created to complete the set. They have immense practical usage of giving an exceptional heat protection.

Designs

The highly elegant cotton pot holders can be created in innumerable styles to provide grace. They may have square or round shapes with a rich medley of colour combinations and patterns. They are available in both traditional and modern designs that appeal to the buyers.

Types of Pot Holders

The beautiful collection of cotton pot holders is available in various types such as:

- Hand-woven
- Hand painted
- Embroidered
- Machine Printed.

Kitchen/Hand Towels

Kitchen towel is used for various purposes in the kitchen. These towels are very handy to use. They are not only useful and necessary, but also decorative accents in your kitchen. The kitchen towels should be easily absorbent and washable and durable. Kitchen towel comes in different sizes, according to the purpose it has to serve.

Made of linen, cotton, kitchen towels exude refreshing coolness, in hot weather and on cold days, enfold with pleasant warmth. Being fully washable and dryable, the kitchen towels are very cheery and decorative and make a nice addition to the kitchen.

They need to be placed close at hand for drying dishes and just-washed hands. These towels are smaller than bath towel and since also used for drying one's hands after washing them, kitchen towels are also known as hand towels.

Designs

The kitchen towels posses innovative designs and excellent colour combinations. They stand out for creative originality in designs, unique skills and mastery of execution and well-thought-out practical uses. Beautiful and attractive flowers, fruits and vegetables as well as other abstract prints are embroidered, printed or woven to kitchen towels. They also come in a wide array of colours. Checked kitchen towels are also very common. Knitted, appliqued, crocheted and striped ones are also available.

Material Used

Kitchen towels are made of various materials like:

- Cotton
- Linen
- Terrycloth
- Microfiber.

Cotton kitchen towels are in high demand in both domestic and international markets. The cotton kitchen towels, available in various colours and prints are both decorative and functional.

Tray Cloth

Versatile and functional tray cloths are used for covering a tray. The use of tray cloth looks elegant and inviting to any guests. These are beautifully pieces of fabric placed on a tray before serving and enhancing the look of the tray also.

These tray cloths are available in a range of intricate designs and colour combinations. Available in various patterns they add dimension to any kitchen linen. Various geometric designs and floral images are printed or embroidered on tray cloths. They are the perfect choice for any festive occasion or even for daily use.

Tray cloth can be:

- Damask tray cloth
- Crocheted tray cloth
- Woven tray cloth
- Embroidered tray cloth
- Hand stitched tray cloth
- Printed tray cloth.

Materials Used

Tray cloths are made of various material like:

- Cotton
- Linen
- Denim
- Paper
- Plastic.

Cotton tray cloths are very popular and in high demand in both domestic and international markets. Available in various colours, prints, and designs, cotton tray cloths can be custom made as per customer's specifications.

Mitten

Mitten is a covering for the hand that encases the thumb separately and the four fingers together. Also known as gloves, mittens are very necessary to use in the kitchen. They are often quickly grabbed for and are adaptable for all the cooking solutions. They help make a decorative statement for kitchens and are functional for a variety of purposes.

Designs

Mittens are made of linen, cotton and othe fabrics. They are made thick and insulated so as to resist heat. They are a must for the kitchen and are available in a number of patterns with distinctive textures and quality. With attractive prints and solid colours, mittens can be enhanced to suit the personal tastes of buyers.

Types of Mittens

The highly appealing mittens crafted out of cotton are available in various types such as:

- Hand-woven
- Hand painted
- Embroidered
- Machine Printed Patterns.

Cotton mittens or any other mittens come in a variety of patterns that includes:

- Solid
- Checks
- Floral
- Geometric
- Abstract
- Provence.

Cheese Cloth

Cheese cloth is a very handy kitchen linen. Made of high density cotton fibre it is a multipurpose linen. It can be used both for domestic as well as commercial purpose.

Types of Cheese Cloth

- Fine Cheese Cloth-Used to drain soften cheese, yogurt, and butter.

- Coarse Cheese Cloth-Used for draining curd, lining cheese shaping moulds and cheese press.

Characteristics of Cheese Cloth

- Made up of high quality woven cotton
- It is washable
- It is reusable.

Applications of Cheese Cloth

- Basting
- Poaching
- Stuffing poultry
- Canning
- Straining
- Wrapping cottage cheese
- Wine making
- Hanging curd.

Dish Clothes

Dishcloth is used to wash dishes and is an essential part of kitchen linen. Usually, dishcloths have a smooth surface and mat luster and feels pleasant to the touch. Dish cloths are generally made of cotton, are very attractive and functional. These dish cloths are often available with a softness that endures even after hundreds of machine washings. Ideal for cleaning, wiping, dusting and washing dishes, cotton dish cloths are very popular and super absorbent.

Designs

Durable and comfortable, the cotton dish cloths add a new dimension to the kitchen and are offered in large ranges and designs. They are easily washable and available in an array of immaculate designs and colour combinations.

Patterns

Cotton dish cloths are available in plain, solids or other

splendid patterns that include: paisleys, florals, animals, geometrics and abstract prints.

Linen Industry

The textile industry in India is one of the largest segments of the Indian economy accounting for one fifth of the country's industrial production. The sector employs around 15 million people and earns a lot of foreign exchange through this industry.

Table and kitchen linen are broadly an important section of the home furnishing industry that falls under the preview of the textile industry.

Manufacturers and exporters in this industry offer a spectacular range of table and kitchen linens including table cloth, towels, napkins, table mats, aprons, mittens, etc.

India is one of the major suppliers of kitchen linens in the world market. Export of handmade cotton table and kitchen linens and other cotton furnishings accounts for a major section of export.

A forerunner in international markets, the Textile Industry in India is widely acclaimed and acknowledged for its superb quality textiles. Total textile exports during April-March 1998-99 were to the tune of US $ 12533.1 million (RS.52720.78 crores). April 2000 to December 2000 has seen a remarkable increase in total exports of textiles at US$9735.2 million (RS.440179.4 million). The main markets for Indian textiles are USA, UAE, UK, Germany, France, Italy, Russia, Canada, Bangladesh and Japan.

Chair Covers

Chair covers sit over the entire chair covering the back, seat and base of the chair. Made of cotton and other fabrics, the beautiful chair covers create an elegant atmosphere that would be remembered for years to come. Cotton fibres are strong and lustrous as well as cool and absorbent. Cotton chair covers are very much in demand. The mesmerizing range and premium quality cotton chair covers are an ideal choice for the buyers, worldwide. Adding cotton chair covers to special events help build the setting, which is unquestionably elegant and appealing.

Designs

Available in multitudes of designs, the cotton chair covers are beautiful accessories that compliment the decor. All chair covers come in many shades of different colours to match the colour scheme that the buyers are looking for plus to complement the room's decor. They can also be custom-designed in accordance with the specifications and demands of different customers.

Applications

The elegant and attractive chair covers are skillfully created in cotton and other fabrics and can be used for special occasions like: weddings, elegant parties, anniversaries, corporate outings or just for any event.

A Uniform Style Statement

Well groomed staff in the hospitality industry not only gives a property or an F&B outlet an edge but is a prerequisite to success. Uniforms or a dress code play an important role in this and is a reflection of the company's business philosophy. By Sayoni Bhaduri.

At a time when international hospitality brands are making a beeline to get a taste of Indian hospitality, they need a way to incorporate the Indian flavour to make their guests feel more comfortable. Uniforms are a foolproof way of bringing in the Indian flavour; this also brings in regional flavour without compromising on the international tastes.

It is however important to remember that the idea has to blend well with the company's ideology, together with the kind of space and feel they wish to create. The need is much more than just incorporating ethnicity. A spokesperson for ITC Welcomgroup, explains why this hospitality major adopted the ideology it did. "The company follows the core idea of providing India to our guests the way no one else can. This basic concept is followed by all our hotels-in the architecture, interior spaces and even the uniforms," she says.

There also has to be the feeling of formality. At a very basic level, uniforms distinguish the guest from the staff. Indian saris are the ultimate in Indian ethnicity and also exude elegance. However, saris may become a hindrance in a few departments like housekeeping and the kitchen.

While some uniforms are meant to look good, the others, especially the ones for the back-end jobs, are meant for comfort and practical uses. This is where the ingenuity of a designer comes in. Sangita Rohira, CEO of the uniform division at AND Designs India led by designer Anita Dongre, says, "Looks are the easier part of designing uniforms, what is more important is the efficiency it gives and its sustainable material." Different divisions and departments have different uniform to distinguish them from other areas and also allow ease of work. The ITC Welcomgroup spokesperson agrees and says, "Comfort, functionality and relevance in other areas are factors that ascertain choice of uniforms."

The Designs

The designs are mostly a collection of the company's ideology, the needs of the hotel and a result of the designers' creativity. While ITC Welcomgroup has its guest relations in regional saris across all brands, including those with international marketing alliances such as with The Luxury Collection and the Sheraton like the Paithani saris in Mumbai and Kanjeevarams in Chennai. Other uniforms have been designed by the Late Barbara Batta Glini, where the inspiration was India but styled in a western accent. The Taj, under its current rebranding strategy, is also looking at a new look and style. With its luxury brands, they have opted for traditional Benares silk saris for their staff.

This initiative is part of the special social responsibility act wherein Taj has selected three villages where 25 master weavers have been rehabilitated and given orders by the company to produce saris according to the designs and specifications given by designer Jay Ramrakhiani. The raw material is being sourced from Karnataka-based Chamundi Silks.

A more urbane look is what designer Anita Dongre has done for the Taj Gateway brand. She says, "We were asked to create something which was refreshing and different from the usual formal look. So we came up with beige suits with red Chinese collars and no ties creating a semiformal look." She adds that a lot of cotton and local block printing techniques were used for the Taj jungle lodge uniforms.

But there are distinctions between what a city-based business hotel and getaway resort might demand. Business hotels need the air of formality allowing limited space for carefree creativity. "Functionality, comfort and relevance of profile are the key factors for deciding clothing. It would be difficult to have men in traditional uniforms in business hotels," says the ITC Welcomgroup spokesperson, adding that the group has a panel of in-house experts who address the issue of practicality keeping in mind things like the texture, colour, etc.

Limited to suits, men's wear in hotels can be quite mundane. But there are options that can be looked into. As a designer, Dongre believes that a lot can be done with men's wear, that too without subtracting from the formal look. "One can add the ethnic touch to men's formal wear with traditional embroidery; it can be done on ties or blazer lapels and even pockets," she says. But this is not all-there is the quintessential Jodhpuri that can sharpen up looks across all quarters. This is validated by the uniforms in ITC's leisure hotels like Agra and Jaipur where the staff does wear thematic uniforms.

It finally boils down to the aspiration value the company wishes to create. But with a little bit of creativity and style can spruce the entire act, empower the employees and create a good impression the guests as well.

Housekeeping Uniforms

At Saxon Uniform Network, Inc.,we keep the comments and suggestions of hotels in mind when we design housekeeping dresses. That's why, in addition to the IN STOCK styles shown on these pages, we can also design a custom housekeeping dress program, especially for you, with the styles, fabrics, and colours you want. At Saxon Uniform Network, Inc. we stock an extensive line of ready made Housekeeping Uniforms, and can also custom make your order, whether you want a completely new look, or just an improvement!

In the Guest Room

- Spend the night in your own guest room. It's the best way to find out if it is comfortable and equipped with what a guest will need. Essentials include a good reading lamp, a box of tissues, an alarm clock, a nightlight, and a mirror.
- Be sure all bed linens are clean and in good condition. Replace anything that is worn, including pillows and mattress covers.
- Clean out the closet and add empty hangers so guests have a place to hang their clothes.
- Some guests like to unpack completely, while others prefer to live out of their suitcases. Prepare for both options by providing an empty drawer and a flat surface for the suitcase.
- Leave an extra blanket out so guests don't have to go searching if they get chilly in the middle of the night.

6

Use of Computer in Hotel Accountancy Systems

Uniform accounts is used by several hotels/restaurants of the same accounting (costing and sales) principle and/or practices. Uniform accounting is thus not a separate technique or method. It simply denotes a situation in which number of hotels/restaurants may use the same accounting (costing and sales) principle in such a way as to produce costs and sales which are of maximum comparability because from such costs and sales, valuable conclusion can be drawn and one hotel can be compared to others. The extent of application of uniform accounting principles depends on the circumstances of each case. Many schemes of uniform accounting system have been introduced in the last century and a few of them are still in use. The most successful uniform system of accounting was the one introduced by the Federation of Master Printers in 1911 and the most successful system in hotel industry was introduced in March 1926 by the Hotel Association of New York City and in September, 1926 the American Hotel and Motel Association of the North America adopted the same and recommended its members to adopt it. The success of Uniform Accounting System depends on the removal of the following difficulties.

1. Existence of Cooperation, mutual trust and a policy of give and take amongst the participating member hotels/ restaurants.
2. Free exchange of Ideas and Technology, knowledge amongst the member hotels/restaurants.

3. Free exchange of information regarding system of costing stocks, depreciation, etc.
4. Absence of rivalry and sense of jealousy amongst the member hotels/restaurants.
5. Use of common heads to record sales of hotel like Room Sale, Food Sale, Beverage Sale, Laundry Income, Telephone Income, Health Club and Swimming Pool Income, etc.
6. Use of common terminology and procedure regarding cost apportionment and cost control.

It may be noted the accounting system of hotels/restaurants may vary widely on the account of the following reasons

1. Size of Business : In a small hotel/restaurant/guest house, the owner with the help of family members may perform most of the function himself and he may use his personal kitchen for preparing food for the guests. Whereas, in large hotels the job is divided amongst departments and sections and cost allocation is required to be done differently.
2. Method of Production : Some small hotels may find it convenient to buy the food and beverage items from outside and sell it to the guests by adding their margin of profit. Whereas, large hotels find it more economical to cook themselves and serve it to guests.
3. Difference in Apportionment : There can be a large degree of difference in the accounting treatment of expenses, different bases of collection, absorption of overheads, method of depreciation, etc.

Where a Uniform Accounting System is introduced there must be some uniformity in the treatment of sales, expenses and general accounting procedures.

The following important matters require uniformity of treatment

1. Sales accounting policy and principle : The heads for different departments and outlets sales must be finalized so that each hotel and restaurant follows the same heads.

This will help in comparing the sales of one hotel with other.

2. General classification of accounts : There must be clear distinction about direct cost, indirect cost, food cost (variable cost), labour head, overheads, etc.
3. Allocation and apportionment of overheads : The hotels/ restaurants should be divided amongst suitable cost centres and the basis for the apportionment and allocation should be fixed so that all members follow the same principles. The overheads of the hotels/restaurants should also be absorbed uniformly.
4. The member hotels and restaurants under uniform accounting system should have the agreement on the following items

a) Method of depreciation and of pricing of material should be adopted.

b) If interest of capital should be debited and if so then on what basis.

c) If notional interest or rent should be charged on land and building owned by the hotel.

d) How wastages, complementary food served to guests and staff should be treated.

e) On what rate overtime, conveyance, etc. should be paid.

Advantages of Uniform Accounting System

The following are the advantages of Uniform Accounting System

1. Transfer : The staff can be transferred from one hotel to the other very easily as due to same accounting system it does not take long for the staff to adjust to the new hotel.
2. Comparison : Since hotels are following the same accounting system so they can be compared amongst each other. One can find out the causes for higher costs or lower sales and can take corrective measure.
3. Buying Shares : General public or financial institutions

can compare the hotels profitability and it helps them in deciding the price. They should pay to buy the equity, take over or to pay as a loan.

4. Lease or Rent : It is easy to decide on the rent or a lease for the hotels/restaurants. Both tenant and owner can study and compare the expenditure and income of various hotels/ restaurants and this will help to decide on the rental value or lease money for the hotel/restaurant on yearly or season basis.

As it has been discussed in the above that it is not easy to introduce Uniform Accounting System. In fact keeping in view, the heterogeneous industry like hotels, airlines, catering, restaurants, clubs, etc. and moreover, they are located at different places and of different sizes and providing different types of services, it becomes more difficult to have a Uniform Accounting System.

In India hotels to save income tax and other taxes do not at times show actual sale; on the contrary at times hotels show more sale then the actual to make the balance sheet look rosier. Due to high depreciation allowed hotel's in spite of showing more sale are able to save income tax and can convert black money to white money. Thus hotels do not follow the Uniform System of Accounting.

The following schedules are accepted by a group of restaurants to have uniformity in the accounting system. These schedules are as follow

- food sale
- beverage sale
- other income
- salary and wages
- employee's benefits
- direct operational expenses
- music and entertainment
- marketing expenses

- energy expenses
- administrative and general expenses
- repairs and maintenance
- rent and rates
- other expenses
- depreciation
- interest
- income tax.

Food Sale : Schedule D 1 for food sale is designed initially to show the number of meals served and amounts by meal period and secondly by dining area. Food sales include sales of tea, coffee, fresh juices, food, bakery products sold at restaurants, room service, banquets, etc.

Beverage Sale : This includes the sale of aerated drinks, canned juices, Beer, Wine, Cocktails, Hard drinks, etc. The beverage sale of bar, room service bar and beverage sale shown by other outlets is included and shown as Beverage Sale.

Other Income : Other income includes income from swimming pool, floweriest shop, health club, income from beauty parlour, etc. Net income means sale less cost of sale is shown as income under the head Other Income.

Income from rentals, interest and dividends earned should be shown as addition to income on the summary statement of income and should not be reported on this schedule.

Salary and Wages : Salary and wages paid to permanent staff, contractual staff and paid to porter for cartage should be included under the head salary and wages. The salary or remuneration paid to the owner is not included under the head salary and wages.

Employee's Benefits : Employee benefits include medical benefit or re imbursement, Contributory Provident Fund or Insurance Fund, Rent Allowance or Rent re imbursement, Leave Travel Concession, Children Education, Free or Subsidized Food, etc.

Direct Operational Expenses : Direct Operational Expenses include all those expenses which are incurred for providing services to the guests like linen, dry cleaning, table ware, kitchen utensils, fuel, stationery, power, etc. But this does not include food cost (variable cost) and direct labour cost.

Music and Entertainment : This includes salary and perks (conveyance, food, insurance, etc.) paid to musicians, rent paid for the equipments, money spend on the booking agent's fees or commission, money paid for procuring films, records, discs, etc. or royalty paid to companies for giving permission to play music in the restaurant or bar.

Marketing Expenses : Marketing expenses include selling, advertising (hoarding, print and electronic advertisement), fees and commissions, salary paid to marketing staff, donations, good will type expenditures, royalties, fees paid to franchisors, money spend on research and development, etc.

Energy Expenses : It includes electricity, heating expenses, water charges, ice and refrigeration supplies, waste removal, etc.

Administrative and General Expenses : The operational expenses like office expenses, stationery used in office, postage, telephone, travelling expenses (travelling not undertaken for the promotion of business), insurance, etc.

Repairs and Maintenance : This includes repair and maintenance of building, equipment like repair and white wash/painting of building, repair of furniture and fixture, repair of kitchen equipments, etc. The money spend on repair should neither increase the production, nor improve the quality of product nor increase the life of asset substantially as this kind of expenditure is considered as capital expenditure and is not debited to repairs and maintenance account.

Rent and Rates : This includes rent and occupation costs, real estate taxes, property tax, building and machinery/equipments insurance, etc. Most of these expense are fixed in nature unless they are linked with sale e.g. the rent can be a certain percentage of sale and will vary depending upon the sale.

Other Expenses : The expenses which are not covered under any of the above mentioned heads are listed under the head other expenses.

Depreciation : In India depreciation is always shown separately as it is a statutory requirement to show profit before depreciation and interest. The Cash Earning Per Share includes the net profit plus depreciation.

Interest : It is very important for investor and general public to know the debt equity ratio of a company. The interest paid on the borrowed money is to be shown separately so the investor can know the financial health of the company.

IncomeTax : Th:? corporate are required to pay income tax on every penny they earn and are shown separately in the books.

Note

Cost of Goods Sold : The cost of raw material of food and beverages sold is termed as cost of goods sold. It is also called as Variable Cost and is deducted from the total sale to know the Gross Profit; some establishments term it as Net Sale as well.

To know the cost of sale the total of raw material consumed is totalled; the other way to find out the cost of goods sold is brought forward of food and beverage products add requisition from stores and deduct the balance in hand at the end of the day. The balance in hand becomes the brought forward on the following day. (To know in detail about cost of goods sold; please refer to 'D' part of this book)

Service Charges : Some hotels charge service charge in lieu of customary payment of tips. The service charge so charged is distributed to the staff and is not shown as sale.

There is no hard and fast rule that each group of company or association has to follow the' above mentioned schedule. The association/group may recommend another schedule depending upon their needs.

The income statement is the detail of revenues and expenses. The income statement provided to suppliers, debtors, creditors, bankers, etc. is different as compare to the income statement prepared for the management.

The income statement provided to management is much more in detail as compare to the income statement presented to suppliers, etc. Usually the income statement provided to management contains last three years revenues and expenses. The gross revenue information detail along with per share revenue like, EPS and CEPS (Earning Per Share, Cash Earning Per Share), profit, etc. is enclosed for the perusal of management and investors.

Income Statement

The summary of all accounts dealing with transactions relating to revenue and expenses is termed as profit and loss account. The account is termed as statement wherein information is accumulated relating to the item or group of items giving information regarding expenses and revenue.

Hotel Income Statements

Net Income = Revenues – expenses

- Revenue results from the sale of goods and services. It also includes interest income, dividend income, and other items reported on the schedule of rentals and other income.
- Expenses are the costs of goods and services used in the process of creating revenue.
- The net income does not necessarily cause a corresponding increase in the business's cash account. Therefore, net income is not cash flow.

Hotel Income Statement Formats

Income Statement Users

a) Internal Users;

- Board of Directors
- General Manager, President or CEO
- Department and/or Division Heads
- Supervisory Positions.

b) External Users;

- Government
- Credit-holders (I.e. Banks, Major Suppliers)
- Potential and Actual Investors.

Income Statement Formats:

- Internal long-form format
- Internal short-form format
- External formats.

1. Internal long-form format presents detailed information to the reader. It encompasses all departments' net revenue, cost of sales, payroll and related expenses, and other expenses and eventually the income or loss engendered from all operations.
2. Internal short-form format is a brief income statement format. It includes shortly the income (or losses) of revenue centres along with undistributed expenses, fixed charges, income tax, and eventually net income.
3. Common-size external format shows the relation-ship of each item in the income statement to net sales (as a percentage)
4. Comparative income statement presents and compares financial data for two or more periods (shown either in dollar amounts or percentages).

Why Income Statement shall be prepared first?

Income Statement shall be first prepared in order to know the Net Income, from which the Company must deduct Dividends Declared to reach Period's Retained Earning which will be accumulated in the Equity Section of the Balance Sheet!

Statement of Retained Earnings

- This very statement represents the lifetime profits (or losses) of a business that have not been declared as dividends to the shareholders. Moreover, this very statement is increased by the net income of the period and decreased by dividends declared for the period.

- Prepared in order to close the period's Net Income and to serve as the amount to be transferred to the Equity Section of the Balance Sheet!
- The Board of Directors' shall first meet and decide whether to distribute Dividends or not. If Dividends would be distributed.
- The Company is not obliged to pay immediately Dividends when they are declared. However, it is compulsory for the Company to pay them on the same Fiscal Year.

Reasons for Making Statement of Income

1. *Debt Servicing Cost :* Income statement helps company to know that whether they are in a position to recover the interest paid on borrowings from bank, market (both secured and unsecured loans) or not.
2. *Return on Investment :* It is very important to know whether the reasonable return is being paid to the investors, share holders both equity and preference or not. The company would also like to maintain different types of reserves like general reserve, capital reserve, special reserve, etc.
3. *Income :* To know Income, Company is making from routine, normal day-to-day operations.
4. *Success or Failure of Management :* Whether company is making reasonable returns from the capital deployed by them. If the returns are better then the competitors then the policies of the management are considered as successful.
5. *Popular :* Whether the goods or/and services offered by the company are popular in the market or not. If the sale is improving or is better then the competitors then it is considered that the services/goods offered are popular.
6. *Price Sensitivity :* The impact on the sale by increasing or reducing the price is known from income statement and this helps management in deciding whether to increase or reduce the rate and by what percentage.
7. *Profit Centred or Volume Centred :* The price sensitivity

helps management in deciding that the policy of the management should be price centred or volume centred. The high volume of sale will give a lower percentage of profit as compare to low volume of sale. The volume of sale will increase if the price of the product is reduced. At times by reducing the price the volume of sale is increased considerably and the management makes more profit even if the percentage profit on sale is lower.

Detailed Study of Income Statement Revenue Earning Departments

1. Lettable rooms
2. Food and Beverage
3. Swimming Pool and Health Club 4. Floweriest and Beauty Parlour
5. Telephone and Secretariat Services 6. Other Operated Departments 7. Rental and Lease Income.

Undistributed Department Expenses

1. Operation Expenses
2. Administrative and General Expenses
3. Salary and Wages
4. Sales and Marketing Expenses 5. Fuel and Energy Cost

Fixed Expenses

1. Rent and Lease
2. Interest
3. Depreciation and amortigation
4. Insurance
5. License Fee.

Balance Sheet-Uniform System of Accounts

The Balance Sheet also known as 'The Statement of Financial Position', contains the assets, liabilities and net worth of a hotel/ company at the end of accounting period or at any given point of time (generally end of the years, half years, quarterly or monthly). If a balance sheet is prepared one day after the previous balance sheet than it will give a slightly different picture about assets, liabilities and net worth. The financial information is useful for different reasons. The following are the important reasons for preparing the Balance Sheet.

1. One can know the current assets like Cash in Hand, Cash at Bank, Stock, Bills Receivable, etc. and compare them with the current liabilities like Sundry Creditors, Bills Payable, Short Term Loans, Outstanding Payments, etc. One can see whether hotel is able to pay the current liabilities or not, or if there is liquid crunch,
2. Most of the assets of the hotels are of fixed in nature. The balance sheet explains about all these assets.
3. Long Term Loans of both secured and unsecured nature is listed on the liabilities side of balance sheet. Higher the debt-equity ratio, more interest burden the hotel has to bear and it affects adversely on the profit of the hotel.
4. Different types of reserves show that whether earning is retained by the hotel for future growth. The capital reserve and special reserve are the indications for the hotels financial stability and capacity to pay for secured and unsecured loans.
5. One can see whether all authorised capital of hotel has been issued and subscribed or not and whether equity capital or. preference capital is authorised, issued and subscribed and if both types of capital are issued then what is the ratio and what is the dividend to be paid for preference shares and if any other conditions are attached to the preference shares.

The balance sheet (Account Form) has been discussed in detail in earlier part of this book. The students may note that in North America the left side of balance sheet is called 'Assets' and right side as 'Liabilities'. Where as, in India the left side is called 'Liabilities' and right side 'Assets'. Balance Sheet (Report form) is discussed in this chapter.

Limitations of Balance Sheet

Though balance sheet is one of the most important instruments of financial accountancy but still it has certain limitation. *The following are the limitations:*

1. It is based on transactions recorded in accordance with GAAP (Generally Accepted Accounting Principles). The land and building is recorded in the balance sheet at cost price, the price of building is depreciated every year and the depreciated value of building like other assets is recorded. The present value of the land might be much more then that of book value of land (cost price of land) but this appreciated value of land can not be shown in the balance sheet so it does not give the real value of assets.
2. The Rupee is depreciating regularly. The imported equipment purchased three years ago might have more value in terms of Indian Rupees but this increased value can not be shown in balance sheet.

These two reasons can be corrected by putting a foot note just below the balance sheet. The three major Indian Hotel Chains viz East India Hotel (E.I.H.-Oberoi), Indian Hotels (Taj Hotels), ITC Hotels (Welcome Group of Hotels) have much more actual value then shown in the balance sheet because the properties purchased many years ago have much more value then the book value shown in the balance sheets. The goodwill is shown in the books only when a price is paid for acquiring the goodwill. The three major Indian hotel chains have acquired goodwill with their own efforts and performance so they are not showing any goodwill in the book. Any buyer who is interested in buying these equities (shares) wants to know the real value of assets and goodwill before taking a final decision.

Contents of the Balance Sheet

Assets:

The Assets of a hotel can be divided into the following parts:

1. Current Assets
2. Fixed Assets

3. Deferred Revenue Expenses
4. Investments
5. Non Tangible and Other Assets.

Current Asset **:** Currents assets are those assets which can be converted to cash at a short time of say six months to one year. Current assets are listed in the order of liquidity. These are:

a) *Cash* : Cash means total cash in hand at Front Office, Restaurant, Bar, Health Club, Swimming Pool, Cashier, Petty Cashier including imprest money sanctioned to all cashiers.

b) *Bank:* Cash balance with all the banks along with the cheques, drafts deposited but not collected as yet and cash being deposited in the bank. From this total, the total amount of cheques issued but not presented as yet for payment is to be deducted.

c) *Sundry Debtors* :They are all those persons to whom credit has been extended and the account department is sending them bills for payment. These sundry debtors are usually those people who have stayed in the hotel and signed at the time of check out or paid through credit cards. In case the hotel is of the view that any part of these debtors might not pay due to any reason then from these debtors expected bad debts are deducted and the net amount is written in the amount column against sundry debtors.

d) *Closing Stock* : Closing stock means the stock of all kitchens and restaurants material whether kept in kitchens/ restaurants or store is recorded in the closing stock.

e) *Bills Receivable* : In case'bills or promissory notes are issued to any person then these are also recorded in the current assets.

f) *Advance Salaries and Other Expenses* : Sometimes hotel pays advance salary to employees for some reason. The rent, insurance premium, commission, etc. might have been paid in advance without being due then this is shown as current assets and is adjusted as and when it becomes due.

Fixed Assets : Fixed assets are those tangible assets, which are beneficial to hotel for more then one year and it must have a substantial value. Some hotels may not consider any assets of less then Rs. 5,000 as assets even if it has value for more then one year. e.g. buckets bought for hotel may have more then one year life but are still not considered as assets because of their low monetary value. Each fixed asset, may be with the exception of land, depreciates due to wear and tear as the time passes. So the depreciation is charged to each fixed asset and the depreciated value of the asset is shown in the balance sheet under the head fixed assets. The following are the fixed assets and are listed in the order of liquidity.

a) *Furniture and Fixture :* The hotels have large assets in the form of furniture and fixture. Each bed room, bath room, restaurant, bar, stores, lobby, etc. have a lot of furniture and fixture fittings.

b) *Machinery:* It includes Kitchen, Bar, Restaurant, House keeping equipments. It also includes cutlery, laundry equipment, centralized heating and air-conditioning, etc.

c) *Land & Building :* If the building is purchased then it must also include the brokerage charges, registration fee and the value of the land and building should be shown separately in the books. But if the building is constructed then the entire material, labour, consultancy, supervisory, architect cost should be debited to building account. If the old building is purchased and is renovated before starting the hotel then renovation cost should also be added to building account.

Deferred Revenue Expenses : Sometimes hotel makes major revenue nature expenditure and it gives a utility to the hotel for more then one year and due to limited profit it is not written off in the financial year when it is incurred. There is no hard and fast rule that what types of expenditure should be treated as deferred revenue expenditure. The following are the most common deferred revenue expenditures

a) *Major Renovation :* A hotel is usually renovated after a few years to stay in the business and to make it more comfortable to guests. A large amount of money is spending on the renovation of the hotel and hotel does not require any major expenditure on renovation for next couple of years. The accountant show a part of the renovation expenditure in current financial year's profit & loss account and the balance is shown as an asset under the head deferred revenue expenditure and is written off in the next three to four years.

b) *Advertisement :* Whenever a new hotel or a new restaurant is opened a large amount is spending on its publicity so that awareness can be created in the market about the new property. Usually this expenditure is of large amount and this advertisement gives benefit to hotel for many years to come and hence the expenditure is shown as deferred revenue expenditure.

c) *Pre-Opening Expenses :* Sometimes hotels make large pre-opening expenses in the form of advertisement, soft opening, etc. and these expenses are also shown as deferred revenue expenses in balance sheet.

Note : 1. Pre-opening expenses can be capitalised.

Major Renovation Expenses can be Capitalised, if Hotel Increases the Tariff after Renovation

Investment: In case hotel has surplus cash and does not have any expansion plan for the time being, decides to invest it in the form of fixed deposits, debentures or buy shares of other public limited company to earn some revenue for the hotel. These investments are bought in the name of the company and are shown in the balance sheet. These different investments are discussed in detail in later part of this book.

Non Tangible & Other Assets : Non tangible are those assets which can neither be seen nor felt as they have no shape but have value like Goodwill, Patent, etc. Other assets are security paid for water connection, Gas connection, Power connection or Bar license or Hotel license fee. When goodwill or patent is bought from another person then only it is shown because one may pay some money towards goodwill, patent fee, etc. But if the goodwill, patent is earned with own efforts of business then it is not shown in the books. It may have a value in the eye of a buyer but it is not shown in the balance sheet.

Liabilities

The amount which is due to others on the date of writing balance sheet is listed under the head liabilities. The total of assets side and liabilities side is always the same. In other words:

Assets = Liabilities + Capital or

Capital = Assets-Liabilities

The liabilities can be divided into four parts

Current Liabilities : Current liabilities are-those liabilities which are to be paid within a year. These are:

a) *Sundry Creditors* :The hotel buys stock and equipment from suppliers and usually does not make cash payment. These suppliers are paid within one month to six months depending upon the terms and conditions and hotel's policy.

b) *Bills Payable: In case a bill was accepted from someone then the value of the* bill is settled in 30 days and is shown as a current liability.

c) *Advance Received :* At the time of room reservation or part booking an advance is received for confirming the booking and is adjusted against the bill as and when it is raised. Till the amount is adjusted, this advance is shown as a liability against advance received.

d) *Unpaid Expenses :* In case some expenses like rent, interest, commission, *salary, etc. is due but not paid as yet is shown as a liability in the balance* sheet. This liability may be paid almost immediately.

e) *Short Term Loans :* Some times hotel takes short term loans to meet the demands of recurring expenses. Usually these loans attract high rate of interest and have to be paid within a year.

f) *Dividend Payable* : The dividend declared but not paid due to unavoidable reasons is listed as a liability in the balance sheet.

***Long Term Liabilities* : These** are those liabilities which need not be paid within one year or in other words it has to be paid after two to five years. These loans are taken for capital expenditure. The hotel must keep this loan amount as low as possible to keep the interest burden. within limits. The long term liabilities are:

a) *Long Term Loans* :.These loans are taken from banks, financial institutions or from public and are to be repaid after two to five years or may be more.

b) *Debentures* : Sometimes hotel issue debentures to collect money from the market for a long term. The debentures are to be paid back in two to four installments in three to ten years and more.

***Reserves & Surplus* :** The hotel does not distribute all its profit to share holders but some profit of it is retained as surplus. The hotel may also earn some money on selling assets or sell shares at premium or may create special kind of reserve for some specific purposes. Whatever may be the reason, the reserve is a cash with the hotel and can be used for the development and expansion. Broadly reserves are of three types:

a) *General Reserve* :The undistributed profit is transferred to reserve account. This reserve is maintained so that hotel can pay dividend on subsequent years even if there is not sufficient profit or this reserve is used for the expansion of business.

b) *Capital Reserve* :This reserve cannot be used for paying dividend to share holders and is created on selling the assets at over and above the book value or by selling shares at premium. This can be used for acquiring assets or for expansion of business.

c) *Special Reserve* :This reserve is created to pdy back certain liabilities which will be due for payment after one to three years. These reserves are created from the profit of the hotel operations.

Capital : The hotels have two types of Share Capital and these are Equity Share Capital and Preference Share Capital.

a) *Equity Share Capital & Preference Share Capital :* Equity shares are the shares which are issued to the share holders. These share holders get profit only if there is surplus earning from the business. The preference sháre holders get a minimum of certain fixed dividend even' if there is no earning.

The other Types of Capital are;

i) *Authorised Share Capital :* It is that amount of capital which a hotel can issue to the public. The hotel may or may not issue all the capital it is authorised to issue. In case the hotel wants to increase the authorised capital then it has to obtain the approval of share holders and intimate the decision of share holders to SEBI.

ii) *Issued Share Capital :* It is that amount of capital which is issued to the public through prospectus. The Board of Director may or may not issue all the authorised capital to the public for subscription.

iii) *Subscribed Capital :* All the issued capital may or may not be subscribed by the public. But if public does not subscribe 90% of the issued capital within the stipulated time then Board of Directors are required to return the money to subscribers and no share can be allotted.

Responsibility Accounting

A hospitality business with several departments, each with the responsibility for controlling its own costs and with its department head accountable for the departmental profit achieved, is practicing what is known as responsibility accounting.

Responsibility accounting is based on the principle that department heads or managers should be held accountable for their performance and the performance of the employees in their department. There are two objectives for establishing responsibility centres:

1. Allow top-level management to delegate responsibility and authority to department heads so they can achieve departmental operating goals compatible with the overall establishment's goals.
2. Provide top-level management with information (generally of an accounting nature) to measure the performance of each department in achieving its operating goals.

Within a single organization practicing responsibility accounting, departments can be identified as cost centres, revenue centres, profit centres, or investment centres. A cost centre is one that generates no direct revenue (such as the maintenance department). In such a situation, the department manager is held responsible only for the costs incurred.

Some establishments also have revenue centres. These departments receive sales revenue, but have little or no direct costs associated with their operation.

For example, a major resort hotel might lease out a large part of its floor space to retail stores. The rent income provides revenue for the department, all of which is profit.

A profit centre is one that has costs but also generates revenue that is directly related to that department. The rooms department is an example where the manager is responsible for generating revenue from guest room sales. The manager of a profit centre should have some control over the sales revenue it can generate. Thus, profit centres are responsible for both maximizing revenue and minimizing expenses, which, in turn, maximizes departmental profit. Each profit centre manager or department head can then be measured on how well profit was maximized while continuing to maintain customer service levels established by top-level management.

In both cost and profit centres, a key question is, what costs should be assigned to each centre? Generally, only those costs that are directly controllable by that centre's department head or manager are assigned.

The final type of responsibility centre occurs in a large or chain organization with units located in several different towns or cities. Each unit in the organization is given full authority over how it operates and is held responsible for the results of its decisions. In a large organization such as this, each unit is said to be *decentralized* and units are sometimes referred to as investment centres. Investment centres are measured by the rate of return their general managers achieve on the investment in that centre.

Transfer Pricing

In some chain organizations, products are transferred from one unit to another.

For example, in a multiunit food organization, raw food ingredients might be purchased and processed in a central commissary before distribution to the individual units. A question arises about the cost to be transferred to each unit for the partially or fully processed products. Many different pricing methods are available. It is important that an appropriate pricing method be decided so each unit can be properly measured on its performance.

For example, the transfer price could be the commissary's cost plus a fixed percentage markup to cover its operating costs. Another method might be to base the transfer price on the market price of the products. The market price would be what the receiving unit would have paid if it had purchased the products from an external supplier. In some cases, the market price might be reduced by a fixed percentage to reflect the commissary's lower marketing and distribution costs. Obviously, each user unit would prefer to have the transfer price as low as possible so its costs are lower, and the commissary would prefer to have the transfer price as high as possible to enhance its performance.

Distribution of Indirect Expenses

One controversial issue concerning the income statement is whether the indirect expenses should be distributed to the departments. The problem arises in selecting a rational basis on which to allocate these costs to the operating departments. Some direct expenses might also have to be prorated between two operating departments on some logical basis. For example, an employee in the food department serving food to customers might also be serving them alcoholic beverages. The food department will receive the credit for the food revenue, the beverage department for the beverage revenue. However, it would be unfair for either of these two departments to have to bear the full cost of that employee's wages.

That cost should be split between the two departments, possibly prorating it on the basis of the revenue dollars. Such interdepartmental cost transfers are easily made; they are necessary to have a reasonably correct profit or loss for each operating department for which the appropriate department head is accountable.

One of the arguments in favor of allocating indirect expenses to departments is that, although departmental managers are not responsible for controlling those costs, they should be aware of what portion of them is related to their department since this could have an impact on departmental decision making, such as establishing selling prices at a level that covers all costs and not just direct costs.

When this type of full-cost accounting is implemented in a responsibility accounting system, it allows a manager to know the total minimum revenue that must be generated to cover all costs, even though the control of some of those costs is not their responsibility. Some undistributed indirect expenses can be allocated easily and logically.

For example, marketing could be distributed on a revenue ratio basis. However, if a particular advertising campaign had been made specifically for one department, and it was thought that little, if any, benefit would accrue to other departments, then the full cost of that campaign could reasonably be charged to that one department as a direct cost.

Internal Control

The control is a continuous process. It is a part of routine in all types of organisations, whether small or big. The word 'control' itself is disliked by one and all, nobody likes to be controlled by others no matter how small or big employee he may be.

Definition

"The whole system of control, financial and otherwise, established by the management in order to carry on the business of the enterprises in an orderly and efficient manner, ensure adherence to management policies, safe-guard the assets and secure as far as possible the completeness and accuracy of the records".

Scope/Objectives of the Internal Control

1. To check frauds and thefts.
2. To safeguard the assets of the business from thefts and misuse (cutlery and small equipments).
3. To improve the efficiency.
4. To follow the policies of the management.
5. To improve the quality.
6. To complete the records up to moment.

Essential Features/Types of Internal Control

1. Experienced, Qualified and Trustworthy Personnel
2. Division of Duty
3. Leadership
4. Organisational Structure
5. Sound Practice
6. Authorise Personnel
7. Records
8. Manual Procedure
9. Control
10. Budget
11. Reports
12. Independent Checks:

    1. *Experienced, Qualified and Trustworthy Personnel* : The personnel should be well qualified, experienced and trustworthy and this helps in providing better services than competitors. This also ensures in having a better internal control on pilferages.

2. *Division of Duty* : The duties are segregated to improve the efficiency, quality and for controlling the pilferage.
3. *Leadership* : Board of Directors, General Manager and other managers and supervisors must lead the person by communicating the policies of the hotel to one and all and encourage the personnel to have the best out put and control.
4. *Organisational Structure* : The Chain of hotels or hotel as the case may be must have a clear organisational structure and the personnel must know from whom to take orders and to whom to report.
5. *Sound Practice* : These are policy measures generally set up and implemented by the board of directors and other senior executives in order to create an environment which facilitates internal control.
6. *Authorise Personnel* : The management must authorize clearly the personnel for taking certain decision. For example: a person should be authorised to extend discount, cancel a bill, extend complementary food/ room, etc.
7. *Records* : The records must be maintained to ensure internal control The records like guest registration cards, bills, K.O.T.'s, control sheets, etc. are not only maintained, checked, verified, but are also stored for future references.
8. *Manual Procedures* : Each job should be reduced to writing. Log books must be maintained in each department. The Manual Procedures should list the details of each position including how and when to perform each task.
9. *Control* : Control includes security services and measures for protecting assets, *(253)* stores, guest's valuables, etc. The security services, as far as possible, must be hired from professionals.
10. *Budget* : The Budgets like short term, long term, specific budgets, etc. must be made for sale, cost, production,

etc. The budgets must be achievable but not achievable so easily. The goals of the hotel must be clearly mentioned and the goals must be made not only for sale, cost, etc. but must also be made for controlling pilferages.

11. *Reports* : For each job reports must be made and circulated among the executives of the hotel for information and control.
12. *Independent Checks* : The personnel responsible for performing the jobs should not be asked for the internal checks but internal checks must be performed by different personnel either from the permanent personnel employed in the hotel or some times may be hired from out side.

The internal control is all the more important in hospitality industry. In normal business houses; the sale is carried out for a limited period of eight to ten hours a day and almost all the sale is made from a sale counter managed by the owner himself or by his confident.

But in Hotel Industry, the cash as well as credit sale is made from various outlets and that too 24 hours a day and 365 days a year. At hotels we sell different kind of food and beverage products both produced at various kitchens of the hotel end procured from outside. We also sell various types of services like health club, swimming pool, beauty parlour, secretariat services, telephone services, and travel services and so on. These sales are made to both in house guests and outsiders. Keeping in view the above facts it becomes very important that we have an affective control over these outlets sales. It is not always possible to have a management eye watching cashiers and other staff members engaged in selling various services, presenting check (bill), settling bills and returning back the balance and receipts.

To ensure that staff does not get tempted to pilferage the cash sales, certain control procedures are developed for the restaurant/bar/other departments sales. The instruments used for the Food and Beverage Service Control are as follows;

1. Kitchen Order Ticket (K.O.T.)
2. Restaurant Check.
3. Restaurant Sales Summary Sheet.
4. Kitchen Summary Sheet.
5. Guest Weekly Bill.
6. Visitor's Tabular Ledger (V.T.L.).

Kitchen Order Ticket (K.O.T.)

The four copies of K.O.T. are made. The order is taken by the captain on K.O.T. The original copy of the K.O.T. is given to Aboyer (Barker) to place the order. After the food has been picked up by the pick-up waiter, this copy of the K.O.T. is kept in the locked K.O.T. Box, which is taken by the control department at the end of the day or shift for control purposes. The first carbon copy is given to cashier so that he can make the check. The second carbon copy is given to pick up waiter so that he can pick up the food from the kitchen. The last copy is kept at the side board (dummy waiter) for the reference of captain or stewards and this helps in service.

Restaurant Check

Restaurant Check is either prepared by cashier or waiter but is usually priced and totalled by cashier. To pick-up the food, the check is shown by pick up waiter and the check items are ticked by barker before giving the food. On demand, all the four copies of the check are presented to the guest, either he pays'in cash or he signs and puts his name and room number or he settled his bill through credit card or debit card. If he pays in cash than the original copy of the check is returned to him with the stamp of paid and cashiers signature as a receipt, but in case he signs as a resident or as a credit card holder than original copy is send to front office and the first carbon copy is given to the guest for his reference. The second carbon copy is send to accounts department and the third, carbon copy is for control department.

In case a restaurant check is lost by the waiter than he is liable to pay Rs. 1,000 as a fine along with the price of the check (The check's price can be ascertained with the help of K.O.T.) In case a check is lost by the cashier then he is liable to pay the fine instead of waiter. When a check is issued to the waiter, he is required to sign in the Restaurant's sales summary sheet and when he returns the check to cashier he takes the stub duly signed by the cashier as a proof that he has returned the check to the cashier.

Restaurant Sales Summary Sheet

On this summary sheet cashier maintains the complete record of restaurant sales. When he issues a check to pick up waiter, he gets his signature and when he (waiter) returns the check to the cashier than the lower perforated portion of the check (stub), along with cashier's signature and stamp, is returned to the waiter and this is his proof that he has returned the check to the cashier.

In case this check is lost than the responsibility is fixed on cashier or waiter and who-so-ever is held responsible, is required to pay the price of the check and a fine of Rs. 1,000. The restaurant sales summary sheet is prepared in duplicate and a copy each is send to the accounts department and control department.

In case guest settles his bill in cash than the amount received is shown in the cash column and discount allowed is shown in the discount column. In case the guest settles his bill by signing (either as a hotel resident or as a credit card/debit card holder) than the total amount is shown in the ledger column and in the remarks column the Room Number, Name of the Guest, Credit Card Number/Debit Card Number and other details are entered. Cashier signs in the Signature column.

Kitchen Summary Sheet

The Chef prepares a Kitchen Summary Sheet with the help of K.O.T's. This is also known as **Kitchen Cost Sheet.** This summary sheet is prepared in duplicate and a copy each is send to the Accounts Department and the Control Department.

Guest Weekly Bill

For each resident of the hotel a guest weekly bill/guest bill is prepared. All debit and credit vouchers along with room tariff are posted in this bill and as soon as guest desires to check out this bill is presented to him for settlement. For control purposes a copy each of this is send to control department and accounts department. But the original copy, in case of cash payment, is given to the guest as his receipt. In case guest signs the bill than original bill copy is send to the company for collection by accounts department and the bill is transferred to Ledger accounts and transferred to Account Department for collection.

Visitor's Tabular Ledger

For all the hotel residents of a day a Visitor's Tabular Ledger is prepared. It is also known as Day Book. For every day a new ledger is prepared. On this ledger the room rent and all the vouchers for all the guests are recorded. The Visitor's Tabular Ledger gives the total sale of the residents of the hotel (but the cash paid by residents in restaurants is not recorded here). A copy each of this ledger is send to the control department and accounts department.

Visitor's Tabular Ledger

In case the hotel has the computerized accounting system than the restaurant sales summary sheet, guest weekly bill, kitchen summary sheet and visitor's'tabular ledger are automatically made and the control department can have their printouts on their computers. In some hotels a separate K.O.T. is not prepared; the restaurant check is prepared by machine/computer. The monitor of kitchen shows the order and a K.O.T. in leaf form is not given to barker. For ordering the food there is no need to show the check because order is only placed through computer if check is prepared.

Cash Control

As it has been already discussed in 'Restaurant Sales Conter I' that cash sales are made at various outlets throughout the day and night. A hotel ay make a couple of lakhs of Rupees cash sale in a day.

A cashier may be tempted to run away with the cash. To have an affective control of cash the hotel's management usually do not appoint a cashier unless and until they are very sure about his credentials and they take minimum of two references. Usually cashiers are rotated very regularly from one outlet to the other and head cashier keeps a watch on them. All the cash collected by cashier is deposited to the front office cashier along with sales summary sheet. The imprest amount given to cashier is checked quite regularly by head cashier/accountant/control department. The cashiers are not allowed to keep imprest money with them but is also deposited/kept at hotel or handed over to the cashier of next shift. All the check books are numbered and in case of any cuttings the checks must be counter signed by the manager. The front office cashier is required to prepare a cash book. All the cash received must be banked. Except front office cashier, who may be required to make petty cash payments on behalf of resident guests against visitor paid out, no other cashier is authorized to pay from the cash sales.

Cash Receipts and Payments/Disbursements

It is very important to control the cash receipts and cash payments/disbursements. No doubt in hotel industry it is becoming more and more common to settle the bills through vouchers/credit facilities extended to regular customers and through credit or debit cards but still a good number of guests settle their bills in cash. Moreover the cash is received throughout the day and night and at various cash counters spread in different parts of the hotel.

Cash Receipts

Cash receipts must be controlled from the point of sale till it is banked. The following steps are followed for its control

1. Checks must be prepared for each cash receipt and a proper receipt must be handed over to the guest.
2. The Checks must be numbered and tearing, cutting or canceling of check must be signed by an authorised manager.
3. All Checks must be entered in the Sales Summary Sheet.
4. The total cash received must be deposited in the bank immediately after the shift is over or instantly when there is cash more then the recommended cash in the cash chest.

The cash should be deposited by each cashier him self or it should be deposited by the Front Office Cashier. But the Front Office Cashier must issue a receipt to each cashier on receiving the cash from them. The cash so received by Front Office Cashier must be shown in the Cash Book.

5. Each cashier should be given a float/imprest for paying balance to guests or for encashing foreign currencies (Only Front Office Cashier is authorised to accept foreign currency from guests). The float so handed over to the cashiers must be checked both at the end of the shift and during the shift (surprise check). The cashier should not be allowed to keep the float with them after the shift is over and the float should be deposited with the Front Office Cashier or should be handed over to the next shift's cashier.
6. The allowances/discounts/complementary should be only extended and signed by the authorised personnel.
7. The un used checks must be kept under lock and key and the serial numbered checks are issued to the cashiers against their signatures.

Cash Payments/Disbursements

This includes control over purchases, expenses and salary payments. As far as possible the cash payments should not be encouraged. All payments must be made by cheques. As far as possible the hotel must avoid making cash payments, however, petty payments may be made, in cash by petty cashier. The cheque must be kept under lock and key and cheque payments must be made after verifying the bills, supply order, purchase order, invoice, store keeper's report, etc. Salary should be disbursed by making a direct payments to the employee's account opened in the hotel's bank. Before making the salary payments the attendance from the department and time office must be taken into account. For larger amount cheques, if possible, two authorized persons must sign the cheque. The cash book must be kept ready up to moment and must be signed daily by an authroised person. The bank reconciliation statement must be prepared on weekly or fortnightly basis.

Types of Internal Control

The following are the main types of internal control

1. Organisation
2. Division of Duties
3. Physical Control
4. Supervision
5. Financial Accuracy.

Organisation : The management must make the organization chart of all the departments. The authorities, responsibilities, reporting to, must be clearly identified; each job must be clearly described and specified. In case of delegation of power, it should be in writing with the approval of superiors. It must be clear to superiors that the authority/power can be delegated to subordinates but the responsibility can not be delegated. The superiors are always responsible for the deed and misdeeds of subordinates. In larger hotels a lot of power is delegated to juniors because one person can not perform all the duties. In smaller hotels the owner himself supervises almost every thing. The organization chart of a hotel may differ from hotel to hotel, depending upon the size of the motel, policy of the hotel, mechanical devices available, etc.

Division of Duties : The duties among different employees must be divided to have an affective control; but in smaller hotels, the broad division of duties may not be possible. For example, in a large hotel the bill clerk and cashier can be separate person; this will have a control of one person over other and less chances of cash pilferage.

Physical Control : In hotels the security is assigned to an outside agency so that security guards and hotel staff do not become friendly. All the departments, when not in operation must be locked and key, after sealing, must be kept with the security officer. The employees must use only staff gate for coming and leaving the hotel. This gate must be manned by a security officer round the clock. Each staff member must be checked physically to ensure that they are not taking away hotel's property, may be by mistake, like match boxes, hand towels, knife, etc. The stores must be locked after normal working hours and no unauthorized person should be allowed to enter. The cash book, keys, cheque books, etc. must be kept in safe custody of responsible person.

Supervision :The supervisors must authorize/approve all the transactions of the hotel. All cutting/over writing must be counter signed. The power of the supervisors must be specified in writing to avoid confusion.

Financial Accuracy: The totals, calculations, pricing of each bill must be checked for its accuracy. The over charging and under charging are very bad for the hotel. The bank account must be reconciled on weekly basis. The checks and K.O.T.'S must be numbered. At the end of every month ledgers must be balanced and trial balance prepared.

With the modern accounting techniques developed, the arithmetic accuracy *is* ensured by machines.

To ensure the affective internal control, the staff must be regularly trained. It is rightly said that training is a continuous process, every employee must be trained for a minimum of 100 hours in a year. The new employees must be imparted training before putting them on the actual job. The old staff knowledge must be updated and in case of shifting to new systems/methods the staff must be trained and motivated. The supervisors and management must ensure that the systems developed by the hotel must be followed by every one and this will always ensure the perfect internal control.

In hotels, a separate internal control department is made under the direct supervision of Chief Controller who reports to General Manager. The primary job of internal control is to help management discharge their responsibilities. The nature and extent of control will depend upon business to business. It will also depend upon nature, size and volume of transactions and the policy of the management.

In spite of the best efforts of management, supervisors and control department, it is never possible to eliminate pilferage altogether. Management always bears in mind the cost of control and the benefits derived from them. Like any other departments operation, internal control department's functions must be regularly reviewed to ensure its *usefulness.*

The following situations must be checked;

1. The staff refuses transfer or promotion.
2. The staff neither wants weekly off nor leaves.
3. The staff has bad evils like gambling, loitering and spending heavily. 4.
   Close relation with suppliers.
5. Close friendship with cashiers, store keeper, kitchen/ restaurant staff.
6. Staff is very close to superiors or control department employees.

Major Types of Frauds

The internal control system is not only designed to prevent and detect fraud, but also to prevent and detect error which is usually more common than fraud. Though it is very difficult to list down all kinds of fraud, in fact every moment some where in the world, a new type of fraud takes place.

Bibliography

Carl H. : *Internet Distribution of European Travel and Tourism Services*, Research Centre of Bornholm, Denmark, 1999.

Coccosis, Harry and Nijkamp, Peter: *Sustainable Tourism Development*, Aldershot, Avebury, 1995.

Cohen, Erik: *Towards a Sociology of International Tourism*, 1972.

Cracknell, H. L.: *Escoffier: The Complete Guide to the Art of Modern Cookery*, New York, John Wiley, 1979.

Cukier, J. : *Tourism Employment in Bali: Trends and Implications*, London: Thompson, 1996.

Donald M.: *Customer Service in the Hospitality and Tourism Industry*, Englewood Cliffs, Prentice Hall, 1994.

Douglas C: *Practical Tourism Forecasting*, Oxford, Butterworth Heinemann, 1996.

Ecotec: *Calderdale: Tourism Impact Study*, Calderdale, ECOTEC/ Calderdale Council, 1990.

Edgell, David L: *International Tourism Policy, New York*, Van Nostrand and Reinhold, 1990.

Elliott, James: *Tourism: Politics and Public Sector Management*, London, Retailed, 1997.

Fayos-Sola, E. : *An Introduction to TEDQUAL: A Methodology for Quality in Tourism Education and Training*, Madrid, WTO, 1997.

Frechtling, Douglas C: *Practical Tourism Forecasting*, Oxford, Butterworth Heinemann, 1996.

Gamble, P. R: *The Educational challenge for Hospitality and Tourism Studies*, Tourism Management, 13, 1992.

Ghimire, Krishna: *The Native Tourist*: Mass Tourism within Developing Regions, London, Earthscan, 2001.

Graham M S: *Language of Tourism*, The, Wallingford, CAB International, 1996.

Gunn, Clare and Var, Turgut: *Tourism Planning*, London, Retailed, 2002.

Hall, C Michael *Tourism Planning: Policies, Processes and relationships*, Harlow, Prentice Hall, 2000.

Jack, G and Phipps, A: *Tourism and Intercultural Exchange: Why Tourism Matters*, Clevedon, Channel View, 2005.

Jakle, John: *Tourist, The: Travel in Twentieth Century North America*, University of North Nebraska, 1985.

Kotler, Philip: *Marketing for Hospitality and Tourism*: New Jersey, Prentice-Hall, 1998.

Labarge, Margaret Wade: *Medieval Travellers: The Rich and Restless*, London, Hamish Hamilton, 1982.

Lock, Dennis: *Project Management*, New York, Wiley, 1996.

Morrell, J. : *Employment in Tourism*, London: British Tourist Authority, 1985.

Norman G.: *Hotel, Restaurant, and Travel Law: A Preventive Approach*, Albany, Delmar Publishers, 1993.

Opperman, Martin and Chon, Kye-Sung: *Tourism in Developing Countries, London*, International Thomson Business Press, 1997.

Richards, G. : *Tourism in Central and Eastern Europe: Educating for Quality*, Tilberg, Tilberg University Press, 1996.

Rogers, H Anthea and Slinn, Judy A: *Tourism: Management of Facilities*, London, Pitman: M & E, 1993.

Schwaninger, M: *Trends in Leisure and Tourism for 2000 - 2010*, Prentice Hall, 1989.

Thomas F. : *Introduction to the Hospitality Industry*, New York, Wiley, 1995.

Van den Berg et al: *Urban Tourism: Performance and Strategies in Eight European Cities*, Aldershot, Avebury, 1995.

Van Harssel, Jan: *Tourism: An Exploration*, New York, Prentice Hall, 1994.

Wahab, S A: *Tourism Management*, Tourism International Press, 1975.

Walle, Alfred H: *Cultural Tourism*: A Strategic Focus, Boulder, Co, Westview Press, 1998.

Index

K

L

M

N

O

P

R

S

T

W

❑❑❑

Anmol

63525 / 151

10/10/12

DN9 | 270

31|3|13